easy Sweaters

50 Knit and Crochet Projects

FamilyCircle
easy Sweaters
50 Knit and Crochet Projects

SoHo Publishing Company
New York

SoHo Publishing Company
233 Spring Street
New York, NY 10013

Editor-in-Chief
Trisha Malcolm

Book Editor
Michelle Lo

Art Director
Chi Ling Moy

Book Manager
Theresa McKeon

Copy Editor
Jean Guirguis

Yarn Editor
Veronica Manno

Technical Editors
Carla Scott
Karen Greenwald

President and Publisher, SoHo Publishing Company
Art Joinnides

Family Circle Magazine
Editor-in-Chief
Susan Kelliher Ungaro

Executive Editor
Barbara Winkler

Creative Director
Diane Lamphron

Library of Congress Catalog-in-Publication Data
Family circle easy sweaters: 50 knit and crochet projects
p.cm.
ISBN 1-931543-11-9
1. Knitting--Patterns. 2. Crocheting--Patterns. 3. Sweaters. I.
Title: Easy sweaters. II. Malcolm, Trisha, 1960-

TT825 .F36 2002
746.43'20432--dc21

Manufactured in China

2001049630

Table of Contents

Easy Does it

Charming knits make a winning statement on the fashion front.

Textured Tunic

for intermediate knitters

A contemporary object of desire. Mari Lynn Patrick's A-line tunic boasts jazzy vertical ribbing. Worked in a purl-garter stitch, it sports full-fashioned set-in sleeves and neckline. "Textured Tunic" first appeared in the Fall '00 issue of *Family Circle Easy Knitting* magazine.

MATERIALS

- *X-Press* by Berroco, Inc., 1¾oz/50g balls, each approx 44yd/40m (wool/acrylic) 20 (22, 24, 26, 28) balls in #3614 olive
- One pair size 13 (9mm) needles OR SIZE TO OBTAIN GAUGE
- Size 13 (9mm) circular needle, 16"/40cm long
- Stitch holders

SIZES

Sized for Small (Medium, Large, X-Large, XX-Large). Shown in size Medium.

FINISHED MEASUREMENTS

- Lower edge 53 (56, 59, 62, 66)"/134.5 (142, 150, 157, 167.5)cm
- Bust 40 (43, 46, 50, 53)"/101.5 (109, 117, 127, 134.5)cm
- Length 28 (28½, 29, 29, 29½)"/71 (72.5, 73.5, 73.5, 75)cm
- Upper arm 15½ (17, 18½, 18½, 20)"/38.5 (43, 47, 47, 51)cm

GAUGE

10 sts and 14 rows to 4"/10cm over rib pat using size 13 (9mm) needles.
TAKE TIME TO CHECK YOUR GAUGE.

RIB PATTERN

(multiple of 4 sts plus 2)
Row 1 (RS) K2, *p2, k2; rep from * to end.
Row 2 Purl.
Rep these 2 rows for rib pat.

BACK

Cast on 66 (70, 74, 78, 82) sts. Work in rib pat for 12 rows.
Dec row 1 (RS) K2, p2tog, rib to last 4 sts, p2tog, k2. Work 5 rows even.

Dec row 2 K2, k2tog, rib to last 4 sts, ssk, k2. Work 5 rows even.
Dec row 3 Rep dec row 2. Work 5 rows even.
Dec row 4 Rep dec row 1. Work 5 rows even. Rep last 24 rows once more—50 (54, 58, 62, 66) sts. Work even until piece measures 18½"/47cm from beg.

Armhole shaping

Bind off 3 sts at beg of next 2 rows.
Next row (RS) P1, k1, SKP, rib to last 4 sts, k2tog, k1, p1. Rep last row every other row 2 (3, 5, 5, 7) times more—38 (40, 40, 44, 44) sts. Work even until armhole measures 8½ (9, 9½, 9½, 10)"/21.5 (23, 24, 24, 25.5)cm.

Neck and shoulder shaping

Bind off 5 (5, 5, 7, 7) sts at beg of next 2 rows, 5 (6, 6, 6, 6) sts at beg of next 2 rows. Sl rem 18 sts to a holder for neck.

FRONT

Work as for back until armhole measures 5 (5½, 6, 6, 6½)"/12.5 (14, 15, 15, 16.5)cm.

Neck shaping

Next row (RS) Work 14 (15, 15, 17, 17) sts, sl center 10 sts to a holder, join 2nd ball of yarn and work to end. Working both sides at once, dec 1 st from each neck edge every other row 4 times—10 (11, 11, 13, 13) sts rem each side. When same length as back, shape shoulders as for back.

SLEEVES

Cast on 26 (26, 30, 30, 34) sts. Work in rib pat for 12 rows. Inc 1 st each side of next row then every 6th row 5 (7, 7, 7, 7) times more—38 (42, 46, 46, 50) sts. Work even until piece measures 17"/43cm from beg.

Cap shaping

Bind off 3 sts at beg of next 2 rows.
Dec row 1 (RS) P1, k1, SKP, rib to last 4 sts, k2tog, k1, p1. Rep dec row 1 every other row 7 (10, 12, 12, 12) times more, then every 4th row 1 (0, 0, 0, 0) time—14 (14, 14, 14, 18) sts.

For XX-Large size only
Dec row 2 (RS) P1, k1, SK2P, rib to last 5 sts, k3tog, k1, p1—14 sts for all sizes. Bind off.

FINISHING

Block pieces to measurements. Sew shoulder seams.

Neckband

With circular needle, pick up and k 56 sts evenly around neck edge, including sts from holders. Join and cont in rib pat as established, (working rnd 2 as knit) for 3"/7.5cm. Bind off in pat. Sew sleeves into armholes. Sew side and sleeve seams.

(See schematics on page 134)

Free and Easy

for beginner knitters

Designed by Veronica Manno, a timeless stockinette-stitched cardigan embodies all the comfort needed after a done day. An unassuming pin closure does the trick on this buttonless classic with set-in sleeves and decorative crochet finishing. "Free and Easy" first appeared in the Fall '01 issue of *Family Circle Easy Knitting* magazine.

MATERIALS
- *Baby* by Tahki Yarns/Tahki•Stacy Charles, Inc., 3$\frac{1}{2}$oz/100g balls each approx 60yd/55m (wool)
  9 (9, 10, 11, 12) balls in #5 lt blue
- One pair size 13 (9mm) needles OR SIZE TO OBTAIN GAUGE
- Size J/10 (6.5mm) crochet hook
- One large decorative safety pin
- Stitch holders

SIZES
Sized for Woman's Small (Medium, Large, X-Large, XX-Large). Shown in size Medium.

FINISHED MEASUREMENTS
- Bust 38 (40, 45, 48, 51)"/96.5 (101.5, 114, 122, 129.5)cm
- Length 23 (23$\frac{1}{2}$, 24, 24$\frac{1}{2}$, 25)"/58.5 (59.5, 61, 62, 63.5)cm
- Upper arm 14$\frac{1}{2}$ (15$\frac{1}{4}$, 16, 17, 17$\frac{1}{2}$)"/37 (39, 40.5, 43, 44.5)cm

GAUGE
10 sts and 14 rows to 4"/10cm over St st using size 13 (9mm) needles.
TAKE TIME TO CHECK YOUR GAUGE.

BACK
Cast on 48 (50, 56, 60, 64) sts. K2 rows. Then cont in St st until piece measures 15"/38cm from beg, ending with a WS row. P 1 row on RS (for ridge at yoke).

Armhole shaping
Bind off 3 (3, 4, 4, 4) sts at beg of next 2 rows. Bind off 2 sts at beg of next 0 (0, 2, 2, 4) rows. Dec 1 st each side every other row 3 (3, 3, 4, 3) times—36 (38, 38, 40, 42) sts. Work even until armhole measures 7$\frac{1}{2}$ (8, 8$\frac{1}{2}$, 9, 9$\frac{1}{2}$)"/19 (20.5, 21.5, 23, 24)cm.

Shoulder and neck shaping
Bind off 11 (11, 11, 12, 13) sts at beg of next 2 rows. Sl center 14 (16, 16, 16, 16) sts to a holder for back neck.

LEFT FRONT
Cast on 24 (25, 28, 30, 32) sts. K 2 rows. Then cont in St st until piece measures 15"/38cm from beg, end with a WS row. P 1 row on RS (for ridge at yoke).

Armhole shaping
Next row (RS) Bind off 3 (3, 4, 4, 4) sts, k to end. Cont to bind off at armhole edge 2 sts 0 (0, 1, 1, 2) times, dec 1 st every other row 3 (3, 3, 4, 3) times—18 (19, 19, 20, 21) sts. Work even until armhole measures same as on back.

Shoulder shaping
Next row (RS) Bind off 11 (11, 11, 12, 13) sts for shoulder, sl rem 7 (8, 8, 8, 8) sts to a holder for collar.

RIGHT FRONT
Work as for left front reversing all shaping.

SLEEVES
Cast on 22 (22, 22, 24, 24) sts. K 1 row (on WS). Then, cont in St st, inc 1 st each side every 4th row 0 (2, 2, 2, 4) times, every 6th row 7 (6, 7, 7, 6) times—36 (38, 40, 42, 44) sts. Work even until piece measures 16$\frac{1}{2}$ (17, 17, 17, 17)"/42 (43, 43, 43, 43)cm from beg.

Cap shaping
Bind off 3 sts at beg of next 2 rows, 2 sts at beg of next 2 rows. Dec 1 st each side every other row 3 (4, 5, 6, 7) times. Bind off 3 sts at beg of next 4 rows. Bind off rem 8 sts.

FINISHING
Block pieces to measurements. Sew shoulder seams.

COLLAR
From RS, work across sts from holders and pick up and k 3 sts at each shoulder seam—34 (38, 38, 38, 38) sts. Work in St st, inc 1 st each side every other row 5 times—44 (48, 48, 48, 48) sts. Work even until collar measures 5"/12.5cm. Bind off. Sew sleeves into armholes. Sew side and sleeve seams. With crochet hook, work an edge of sc evenly along center fronts and all around collar edges. Use safety pin to close front at yoke edge.

(See schematics on page 134)

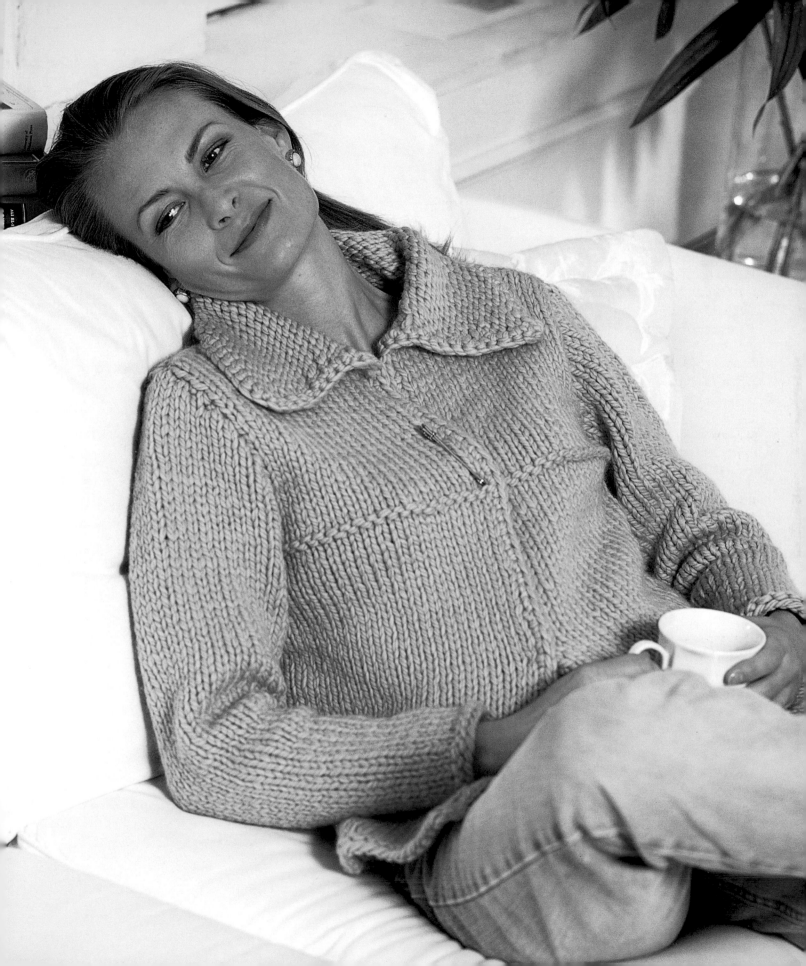

Purple Haze

for beginner knitters

Lend hand-dyed color to a plush, quick-and-easy, stockinette-stitched pullover with raglan sleeves and crochet edges. The multiple yarns of smooth and matte piles create extraordinary lushness. "Purple Haze" first appeared in the Fall '97 issue of *Family Circle Easy Knitting* magazine.

MATERIALS

- *Hand Dyed Zanziba* by Colinette/Unique Kolours, 3¹/₂oz/100g skeins, each approx 104yd/94m (wool/viscose/nylon)
  4 skeins in #83 lilac (A)
- *Hand Dyed Fandango* by Colinette/ Unique Kolours, 3¹/₂oz/100g skeins, each approx 110yd/100m (cotton)
  4 skeins in #83 lilac (B)
- Size 19 (16mm) circular needle 32"/81cm long, OR SIZE TO OBTAIN GAUGE
- Size J (6mm) crochet hook

SIZES
One size fits all.

FINISHED MEASUREMENTS
- Bust 47¹/₂"/121cm
- Length 23"/58.5cm
- Width at upper arm 20"/50cm

GAUGE
8 sts and 10 rows to 5"/13cm in St st using size 19 (16 mm) circular needle and 1 strand each of A and B held tog.
TAKE TIME TO CHECK YOUR GAUGE.

STITCHES USED
Stockinette stitch (St st)
Row 1 (RS) Knit.
Row 2 (WS) Purl. Rep rows 1 and 2 for St st.
Note
Work with one strand each of A and B held tog throughout.

BACK
With size 19 (16mm) circular needle and 1 strand each of A and B held tog, loosely cast on 38 sts.
Next row (WS) Work in St st, working back and forth as with straight needles, beg with a purl row. Cont in St st until a total of 21 rows have been worked. End with a WS row.

Armhole shaping
Bind off 2 sts at beg of next 2 rows—34 sts.
Next row (RS) Dec 1 st each side every other row 11 times—12 sts. Purl 1 row. (A total of 45 rows worked.) Bind off.

FRONT
Work as for back. Work armhole decs until 18 sts rem. Purl 1 row.
Neck shaping
Next row (RS) K2tog, k5, join a 2nd skein of each yarn and bind off center 4 sts, k5, k2tog. Working both sides at once, dec 1 st each side, AT SAME TIME, dec 1 st at each neck edge on the next 2 rows. Work 1 row even, dec 1 st at neck edge of next row. Work 1 row even—1 st. Bind off.

SLEEVES
With size 19 (16mm) circular needle and 1 strand each of A and B held tog, loosely cast on 20 sts. Inc 1 st each side every 4th row 6 times—32 sts. Work even until piece measures 14¹/₂"/37cm from beg.
Armhole shaping
Dec 1 st each side every other row 11 times—10 sts. Dec 1 st each side of next 3 rows—4 sts. Bind off.

FINISHING
Sew side seams. Sew sleeve seams. Sew raglan sleeves to body. With size J (6mm) crochet hook and 1 strand of A, work 1 row sc and then 1 row backward sc around neck edge, easing in as desired.

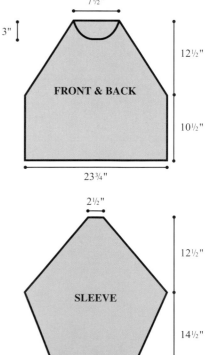

Crochet Chic
for beginner crocheters

Simple shaping and stitching makes this vibrant sweater a fabulous fashion statement. Mari Lynn Patrick's popcorn-stitched tunic exhibits a stand up collar and side slits for a relaxed fit. "Crochet Chic" first appeared in the Fall '98 issue of *Family Circle Easy Knitting* magazine.

MATERIALS
- *Jiffy* by Lion Brand Yarn Co., 3oz/85g balls, each approx 135yd/121m (acrylic)
  9 (9, 10, 11) balls in #113 scarlet
- Size K/10½ (7mm) crochet hook OR SIZE TO OBTAIN GAUGE

SIZES
Sized for Small (Medium, Large, X-Large, XX-Large) Shown in size Medium.

FINISHED MEASUREMENTS
- Bust 35 (37, 40, 42)"/89 (94, 101.5, 106.5)cm
- Length 27½ (27½, 28½, 29½)"/70 (70, 72.5, 75)cm
- Upper arm 15 (15, 16¼, 18¾)"/38 (38, 41, 47.5)cm

GAUGE
6½ pat sts and 8 rows to 4"/10cm over popcorn pat st using size K/10½ (7mm) hook. TAKE TIME TO CHECK YOUR GAUGE.

POPCORN PATTERN STITCH
Chain very loosely, any number of chs.

Row 1 Yo and draw up a lp in 4th ch from hook, yo and draw up another lp in same ch, yo and draw through all 5 lps on hook, ch 1 to fasten, *yo and draw up a lp in next ch, yo and draw up another lp in same ch, yo and draw through all 5 lps on hook, ch 1 to fasten (1 popcorn pat st); rep from * to end. Ch 3, turn.

Row 2 *Yo and draw up a lp in sp between next 2 popcorn sts, yo and draw up another lp in same sp, yo and through all 5 lps on hook, ch 1 to fasten; rep from * end with 1 popcorn st in t-ch. Ch 3, turn.

Rep row 2 for popcorn pat st.

BACK
Ch 39 (41, 43, 45) very loosely. (It is very important to ch loosely to keep edge flat.) Work in popcorn pat st on 36 (38, 40, 42) pat sts for 8 rows or 4"/10cm from beg.

Next (Dec) row Yo and draw up a lp in next sp, yo and through 2 lps, then in next sp [yo and draw up a lp] twice for popcorn pat st, yo and through all 6 lps on hook for 1 pat dec, work in pat to last 2 sps, work 1 pat dec. Rep this dec row every 8th row 3 times more—28 (30, 32, 34) pat sts. Work even until piece measures 20½"/52cm from beg.

Armhole shaping
Rep dec row over next 4 rows—20 (22, 24, 26) pat sts. Work even until there are a total of 14 (14, 16, 18) rows in armhole and armhole measures 7 (7, 8, 9)"/18 (18, 20.5, 23)cm. Fasten off.

FRONT
Work same as back.

SLEEVES
Note
Sleeves are worked from shoulder down to cuff. Sew shoulder seams for 4 (5, 6, 7) sts. Working into side of each row around armhole, including armhole shaping rows, work 28 (28, 32, 36) pat sts around armhole edge. Next row Work in pat st, dec 4 (4, 6, 6) pat sts evenly spaced—24 (24, 26, 30) pat sts. Work even for 4 (4, 4, 2) more rows. Dec 1 pat st each side of next row and rep every 6th row 4 (4, 4, 6) times more—14 (14, 16, 16) pat sts. Work even until sleeve measures 20½ (20½, 21, 21½)"/52 (52, 53, 54.5)cm from shoulder. Work 1 row sl st in back lps only. Fasten off.

FINISHING
Sew side seams leaving first 4"/10cm free for side slit. Sew sleeve seams.

Collar
Collar is worked around neck edge, only worked back and forth in rows. Row 1 Join at one shoulder, work 1 pat st at joining, work 12 pat sts across neck, 2 pat sts at shoulder, 12 pat sts across neck, 1 pat st at shoulder—28 pat sts. Join, ch 3, turn. Working back and forth, work 3 more rows. Work 1 row sl st in back lps only. Fasten off.

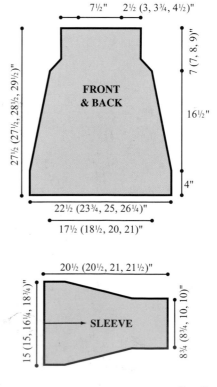

Double Cross

for intermediate knitters

Give a new spin to a simple pullover by alternating bands of stockinette stitch with classic cables. This twist on tradition, designed by Veronica Manno, features side slits, set-in sleeves, and edges finished in a garter stitch. "Double Cross" first appeared in the Winter '97/'98 issue of *Family Circle Easy Knitting* magazine.

MATERIALS

- *Polar* by Rowan, 3¹/₂oz/100g balls, each approx 109yd/100m (wool/alpaca/acrylic) 12 (12, 14, 15) balls in #645 winter white
- One pair each sizes 8 and 9 needles (5 and 5.5mm) needles OR SIZE TO OBTAIN GAUGE
- Cable needle

SIZES

Sized for Small (Medium, Large, X-Large, XX-Large) Shown in size Medium.

FINISHED MEASUREMENTS

- Bust 38 (43, 49, 54)"/96.5 (109, 124.5, 137)cm
- Length 26 (26, 27¹/₂, 27¹/₂)"/66 (66, 70, 70)cm
- Width at upper arm 15 (15, 18, 18)"/38 (38, 45.5, 45.5)cm

GAUGE

19 sts and 22 rows to 4"/10cm over rib and cable pat using larger needles.
TAKE TIME TO CHECK YOUR GAUGE.

STITCHES USED

Rib and cable pattern

(multiple of 13 sts plus 7)
Row 1 (RS) P2, k3, *p2, k6, p2, k3; rep from *, end p2.
Rows 2 and all even rows K2, p3, *k2, p6, k2, p3; rep from *, end k2.
Rows 3 and 7 Rep row 1.
Row 5 P2, k3, *p2, sl next 3 sts to cn and hold to back, k3, k3 from cn (6-st cable), p2, k3; rep from *, end p2.
Row 8 Rep row 2.
Rep rows 1-8 for rib and cable pat.

BACK

With smaller needles, cast on 95 (108, 121, 134) sts. K 8 rows. Change to larger needles.
Row 1 (RS) K5, *p1 into back and front of next st (for inc-1p), p1, k3, inc-1p in next st, p1, k6; rep from *, end last rep k5 instead of k6—109 (124, 139, 154) sts.
Row 2 and all even rows K5, *k3, p3, k3, p6; rep from *, end last rep k5 instead of p6.
Row 3 K5, *p3, k3, p3, k6; rep from *, end last rep k5 instead of k6.
Row 5 K5, *p3, k3, p3, sl next 3 sts to cn and hold to back, k3, k3 from cn (6 st cable); rep from *, end last rep k5 instead of 6 st cable.
Rows 7, 9 and 11 Rep row 3.
Row 12 Rep row 2.
Rows 13-18 Rep rows 5-10 once. Piece measures approx 4¹/₄"/11cm from beg. End of side slit.
Row 19 (RS) P2, k3, *p2tog, p1, k3, p2tog, p1, k6; rep from *, end last rep k3, p2 instead of k6—95 (108, 121, 134) sts.
Row 20 and all even rows K2, p3, *k2, p3, k2, p6; rep from *, end last rep p3, k2, instead of p6.
Row 21 P2, k3, *p2, k3, p2, 6-st cable; rep from *, end last rep k3, p2 instead of 6-st cable.
Rows 23, 25 and 27 P2, k3, *p2, k3, p2, k6; rep from *, end last rep k3, p2 instead of k6.
Rep rows 20-27 for rib and cable pat until piece measures 17¹/₂"/44.5cm from beg.

Armhole shaping

Next row (RS) Dec 1 st at beg and end of row. Work 1 row even. Rep last 2 rows 4 times more—85 (98, 111, 124) sts. Work even until armhole measures 7¹/₂ (7¹/₂, 9, 9)"/19 (19, 23, 23)cm.

Neck shaping

Next row (RS) Work 30 (36, 42, 48) sts, join 2nd ball of yarn and bind off center 25 (26, 27, 28) sts, work to end. Working both sides at once, bind off 3 sts from each neck edge twice. When armhole measures 8¹/₂ (8¹/₂, 10, 10)"/21.5 (21.5, 25.5, 25.5) cm, bind off rem 24 (30, 36, 42) sts each side for shoulders.

FRONT

Work as for back until armhole measures 6 (6, 7¹/₂, 7¹/₂)"/15.5 (15.5, 19, 19)cm.

Neck shaping

Next row (RS) Work 33 (39, 45, 51) sts, join 2nd ball of yarn and bind off center 19 (20, 21, 22) sts, work to end. Working both sides at once, bind off 3 sts from each neck edge 3 times. When same length as back, bind off rem sts each side for shoulders.

SLEEVES

With smaller needles, cast on 34 (34, 43, 43) sts. K 8 rows, inc 1 st each side of last (WS) row—36 (36, 45, 45) sts. Change to larger needles.

(Continued on page 134)

Block Party

for beginner knitters

Designed by Jean Guirguis, this sumptuous cowl-neck pullover is knitted with two strands of complementary shaded cotton and rayon chenille yarns delivers glorious colors and terrific texture. "Block Party" first appeared in the Winter '98/'99 issue of *Family Circle Easy Knitting* magazine.

MATERIALS

■ *Framework Cotton Chenille* by Colinette/Unique Kolours, 3½oz/100g hanks, each approx 216yd/200m (cotton)
  1 (1, 2) hanks in pale blue (A)
  1 hank each in dk plum (B), claret (C), pale olive (D), dk olive (E) and ochre (F)
■ *Isis* by Colinette/Unique Kolours, 3½oz/100g hanks, each approx 108yd/100m (viscose)
  2 hanks each in #118 velvet damson (G), #116 plum (H), #117 velvet bilberry (I), #113 lt olive (J), #114 olive (K) and #112 gold (L)
■ One pair size 13 (9mm) needles OR SIZE TO OBTAIN GAUGE

SIZES

Sized for Small (Medium, Large). Shown in Size Medium.

FINISHED MEASUREMENTS

■ Bust 44 (46, 48)"/111.5 (117, 122)cm
■ Length 26 (27, 28)"/66 (68.5, 71)cm
■ Upper arm 15 (16, 17)"/38 (40.5, 43)cm

GAUGE

9 sts and 12 rows to 4"/10cm over St st using 2 strands of yarn and size 13 (9mm) needles. TAKE TIME TO CHECK YOUR GAUGE.

Note

Work with one strand of Chenille combined with one strand of Isis throughout. Twist yarns tog at block color changes to prevent holes in work.

BACK

With size 13 (9mm) needles and 1 strand of Chenille and Isis held tog, cast on the foll way: 16 (17, 18) sts in B and H, 18 sts in A and G, and 16 (17, 18) sts in C and I for a total of 50 (52, 54) sts. Cont in color blocks as established for 20 (21, 22) rows. Then cont to work color block pat in same number of sts for each block as foll: 20 (21, 22) rows in colors F and L, D and J and F

and L; then in colors B and H, A and G and E and K; then in colors D and J, F and L and C and I to end of piece, AT SAME TIME, when piece measures 18½ (19, 19½)"/47 (48, 49.5)cm from beg, end with a WS row.

Armhole shaping

Bind off 6 sts at beg of next 2 rows—38 (40, 42) sts. Work even until armhole measures 7 (7½, 8)"/18 (19, 20.5)cm, end with a WS row.

Neck shaping

Next row (RS) Work 11 (11, 12) sts, join 2nd balls of yarn and bind off center 16 (18, 18) sts, work to end. Working both sides at once with separate ball of yarn, bind off 2 sts from each neck edge once. Bind off rem 9 (9, 10) sts each side for shoulder.

FRONT

Work as for back until armhole measures 4½ (5, 5½)"/11.5 (12.5, 14)cm.

Neck shaping

Next row (RS) Work 15 (15, 16) sts, join 2nd balls of yarn and bind off center 8 (10, 10) sts, work to end. Working both sides at once with separate ball of yarn, bind off 3 sts from each neck edge once with separate balls of yarn, 2 sts once, 1 st once. When same length as back, bind off rem sts each side for shoulders.

SLEEVES

With size 13 (9mm) needles and 1 strand of Chenille and Isis held tog, cast on the foll way: 12 (13, 14) sts in B and H, 12 (13, 14) sts in D and J for a total of 24 (26, 28) sts. Cont in color blocks as established for 20 (21, 22) rows. Then cont to work color block pat with only 2 blocks to end of sleeve, work 20 (21, 22) rows in colors C and I and A and G; then in colors D and J and F and L to end of piece, AT SAME TIME, inc 1 st each side every 8th row 5 times—34 (36, 38) sts. Work even until piece measures 17 (18, 19)"/43 (45.5, 48.5)cm from beg. Bind off.

FINISHING

Block pieces lightly to measurements. Sew one shoulder seam.

Turtleneck

With size 13 (9mm) needles and A and G held tog, pick up and k 49 (54, 54) sts evenly around neck edge. Work in St st for 9"/23cm. Bind off loosely. Sew other shoulder and turtleneck seam. Sew sleeves into armholes sewing top 2½"/6.5cm of sleeves to bound-off sts at armholes. Sew side and sleeve seams.

(See schematics on page 136)

Essential Crochet

for beginner crocheters

Don't let the basketweave pattern used for this snappy mock turtleneck fool you for a knit. Cleverly crocheted in a combination of stitches, the addition of rib bands produces a knit effect. Designed by Gail Diven, the "Essential Crochet" first appeared in the Fall '98 issue of *Family Circle Easy Knitting* magazine.

MATERIALS

- *Astra* by Patons®, 1¾oz/50g balls, each approx 178yd/163m (acrylic) 14 (14, 15, 15, 16, 16) balls in #2740 purple
- Size F/5 (4mm) crochet hook OR SIZE TO OBTAIN GAUGE
- Yarn needle

SIZES

Sized for X-Small (Small, Medium, Large, X-Large, XX-Large). Shown in size Medium.

FINISHED MEASUREMENTS

- Bust 36½ (39, 41½, 44, 46½, 49½)"/92.5 (99, 105.5, 112, 118, 125.5)cm
- Length 23½ (24, 26½, 26½, 28, 28)"/59.5 (61, 67, 67, 71, 71)cm
- Upper arm 14½ (15¾, 17, 17½, 19, 19)"/37 (40, 43, 44.5, 48.5, 48.5)cm

GAUGE

19 sts and 12 rows to 4"/10cm in pat st using size F/5 (4mm) crochet hook.
TAKE TIME TO CHECK YOUR GAUGE.

Note

All sc, dc, fpdc and bpdc are referred to as sts.

STITCHES USED

Fpdc

Work from front to back around post of dc of previous row.

Bpdc

Work from back to front around post of dc of previous row.

Dec 1 dc

Over 2 sts, [yo and pull up a lp in next st, yo and through 2 lps] twice, yo and through all 3 lps.

Ribbing Stitch

Row 1 Sc in 2nd ch from hook and each ch across. Row 2 Sc in back loop of each sc across. Ch 1, turn. Repeat Row 2 for ribbing pat.

Pattern Stitch

(multiple of 6 sts plus 3)
Row 1 Dc in each st of ch, turn.
Row 2 Ch 3, turn (counts as first st), work fpdc in next 2 dc, * work bpdc in next 3 dc, work fpdc in next 3 dc; rep from * across. Continue to work row 2 for pat st.

BACK

With crochet hook, ch 89 (95, 101, 107, 113, 119).
Row 1 (RS) Dc in third ch from hook and in each ch across—87 (93, 99, 105, 111, 117) dcs. Work row 2 of pat st until piece measures 14 (14, 15, 15, 16, 16)"/35.5 (35.5, 38, 38, 40.5, 40.5)cm from beg, end with a WS row. Do not ch.

Raglan armhole shaping

Next row (RS) Sl st over first 2 sts, ch 3, dec 1 dc, keeping in pat st, work across to last 4 sts, dec 1 dc, leave last 2 dc unworked—81 (87, 93, 99, 105, 111) sts. Work in pat st as established, dec 1 dc at each side every row until 33 (33, 33, 39, 39, 45) sts rem for back neck. Fasten off.

FRONT

Work as for back until armhole measures 6 (6½, 8, 8, 8½, 8½)"/15 (16.5, 20.5, 20.5, 21.5, 21.5)cm, end with a WS row.

Neck shaping

Cont to work side decs as established, leave center 19 (19, 19, 25, 25, 31) sts unworked. Ch 3, turn. Work in pat st, dec 1 st at neck edge every row and at raglan edge as before until piece measures same length as back. Fasten off. Skip center sts and join yarn. Work right front neck as for left front neck.

SLEEVES

With crochet hook, ch 10. Work ribbing st for 38 (38, 44, 45, 47, 49) rows. Ch 1 and working across long edge of ribbing, work 39 (39, 45, 46, 48, 50) sc evenly spaced. Work row 2 of pat st, inc 1 st each side in pat every 3 (2, 2, 2, 2, 2) rows 15 (18, 18, 19, 21, 20) times—69 (75, 81, 84, 90, 90) sts. Work even until piece measures 17 (17, 18, 18, 18, 18)"/43 (43, 45.5, 45.5, 45.5, 45.5)cm from beg. Work raglan shaping as for back until 15 (15, 15, 18, 18, 18) sts rem. Fasten off.

FINISHING

Block pieces lightly. Sew raglan seams. Sew side and sleeve seams. Sc evenly around neck edge.

Neckband

With crochet hook, ch 19. Work in ribbing st until piece, when slightly stretched, will fit around entire neck edge. Fasten off. Sew narrow edges of neck ribbing together. Sewing through the back loops of each sc st, sew neck ribbing in place.

(See schematics on page 134)

Red Alert

for intermediate knitters

Fun to make, Norah Gaughan's slightly shaped funnelneck pullover with bell-shaped sleeves has high-impact style. It knits up quick and easy with luxurious yarns in reverse stockinette stitches. "Red Alert" first appeared in the Fall '01 issue of *Family Circle Easy Knitting* magazine.

MATERIALS

- *Allagash* by Reynolds/JCA, 3½oz/100g balls, each approx 93yds/85m (wool/nylon) 6 (8, 9, 10) balls in #639 red
- Size 11 (8mm) circular needle, 24"/60cm long OR SIZE TO OBTAIN GAUGE
- One set (5) size 11 (8mm) dpn
- Stitch holders
- Stitch markers

SIZES

Sized for Small (Medium, Large, X-Large). Shown in size Small.

FINISHED MEASUREMENTS

- Bust 36 (38, 42, 46)"/91.5 (96.5, 106.5, 116.5)cm
- Hip 45½ (48, 52, 56)"/115.5 (122, 132, 142)cm
- Length 25"/63.5cm
- Upper arm 13 (14, 16, 17)"/33 (35.5, 40.5, 43)cm

GAUGE

10 sts and 14 rows to 4"/10cm over St st using size 11 (8mm) needles.
TAKE TIME TO CHECK YOUR GAUGE.

Note
Piece is shown in reverse St st. For ease in working, work in St st and turn inside out at completion.

BODY

Cast on 114 (120, 130, 140) sts. Join, taking care not to twist sts on needle. Mark beg of rnd and sl marker every rnd. Work in St st (k every rnd) for 4"/10cm.

Next rnd K57 (60, 65, 70), pm (for side), work to end.
Next (dec) rnd K2, K2tog, work to 4 sts before marker, ssk, k4, k2tog, work to 4 sts before marker, ssk, k2 (4 sts dec'd). Rep dec rnd every 10th rnd 4 times more—94 (100, 110, 120) sts. Work even until piece measures 19"/48.5cm from beg, end last rnd 3 sts before marker.
Armhole shaping
Bind off 6 sts, work to 3 sts before marker, bind off 6 sts, work to end. Place sts on holder.

SLEEVES

With dpn, cast on 35 (35, 40, 40) sts. Join, taking care not to twist sts on needle. Mark end of rnd and sl marker every rnd. Work in rnds of St st for 3"/7.5cm.
Next (dec) rnd K2, k2tog, work to 4 sts before marker, ssk, k2. Rep dec rnd every 10th rnd twice more—29 (29, 34, 34) sts. Work even until piece measures 10 (10½, 11, 11½)"/25 (26.5, 28, 29)cm from beg.
Next (inc) rnd K2, M1, work to 2 sts before marker, M1, k2. Rep inc rnd every 12 (6, 6, 4) rnds 1 (2, 2, 3) times—33 (35, 40, 42) sts. Work even until piece measures 18 (18½, 19, 19½)"/45.5 (47, 48.5, 49.5)cm from beg, end

last rnd 3 sts before marker.
Next rnd Bnd off 6 sts, work to end. Place rem 27 (29, 34, 36) sts on holder.

YOKE

K27 (29, 34, 36) from sleeve holder, k41 (44, 49, 54) from front holder, 27 (29, 34, 36) from 2nd sleeve holder, k41 (44, 49, 54) from back holder—136 (146, 166, 180) sts, place marker for end of rnd.
Next (dec) rnd *K3, k2tog; rep from *, end k1 (1, 1, 0)—109 (117, 133, 144) sts. Work even for 2½"/6.5cm. Next (dec) rnd K2 (0, 1, 2), k2tog, *k3, k2tog; rep from * to end—87 (93, 106, 115) sts. Work even for 2"/5cm. Next (dec) rnd K1 (3, 0, 1), k2tog, *k2, k2tog; rep from * to end—65 (70, 79, 86) sts.
Next (dec) row size L (XL) only K2, *k2tog, k9 (4); rep from *, to end—72 sts.
Work even in St st for 7"/18cm. Bind off 65 (72, 72, 72) sts.

FINISHING

Block pieces to measurements. Turn piece inside out with rev St st showing on RS. Sew underarms.

(See schematics on page 135)

Lace Notes

for beginner knitters

Dress it up or down...Irina Poludnenko's roomy, eyelet-and-rib tunic can top a pair of jeans for kick-back ease or a long flowing skirt for a more elegant effect. "Lace Notes" first appeared in the Fall '98 issue of *Family Circle Easy Knitting* magazine.

MATERIALS
- *Tucson* by Reynolds/JCA, 1³/₄oz/50g balls, each approx 118yd/108m (cotton/acrylic) 11(12, 13, 13, 14) balls in #14 green
- One pair size 6 (4mm) needles OR SIZE TO OBTAIN GAUGE

SIZES
Sized for Woman's Large (X-Large, 1X, 2X, 3X). Shown in size Large.

FINISHED MEASUREMENTS
- Bust 49 (51¹/₂, 54, 57, 59¹/₂)"/124.5 (131, 137, 144.5, 151)cm
- Length 27¹/₂ (27¹/₂, 28, 28, 28¹/₂)"/70(70, 71, 71, 72.5)cm
- Upper arm 16¹/₂ (16¹/₂, 17¹/₂, 17¹/₂, 18¹/₂)"/41.5 (41.5, 44, 44, 46)cm

GAUGE
18 sts and 28 rows to 4"/10cm over all pat sts using size 6 (4mm) needles.
TAKE TIME TO CHECK YOUR GAUGE.

STITCHES USED
Pattern Stitch #1
(multiple of 7 sts plus 2)
Row 1 (RS) K1, *k4, p3; rep from *, end k1.
Row 2 K1, *yo, k3tog, yo, p4; rep from *, end k1.
Rep rows 1 and 2 for pat st #1.
Pattern Stitch #2
(multiple of 6 sts plus 2)
Row 1 (RS) K1, *k3, p3; rep from *, end k1.
Row 2 K1, *yo, k3tog, yo, p3; rep from *, end k1.
Rep rows 1 and 2 for pat st #2.
Pattern Stitch #3
(multiple of 6 sts plus 2)

Row 1 (RS) K1, *k3, p3; rep from *, end k1.
Rep row 1 for pat st #3 (k3,p3 rib).

BACK
With size 6 (4mm) needles, cast on 128 (135, 142, 149, 156) sts. Work in pat st #1 for 11"/28cm. Next (dec) row (RS) K1, *k1, k2tog, k1, p3; rep from *, end k1—110 (116, 122, 128, 134) sts. Cont in pat st #2 until piece measures 15¹/₂"/39.5cm from beg. Then, cont in pat st #3 (k3, p3 rib) until piece measures 16¹/₂"/42cm from beg.
Armhole shaping
Cont in rib pat, bind off 8 sts at beg of next 2 rows, 3 sts at beg of next 2 rows, 2 sts at beg of next 2 rows, dec 1 st each side every other row 2 (3, 3, 3, 4) times—80 (84, 90, 96, 100) sts. Work even until armhole measures 10 (10, 10¹/₂, 10¹/₂, 11)"/25.5(25.5, 26.5, 26.5, 28)cm.
Neck and shoulder shaping
Bind off 8 (8, 10, 11, 10) sts at beg of next 2 rows, 8 (9, 9, 10, 11) sts at beg of next 4 rows and AT SAME TIME, bind off center 24 (24, 26, 26, 28) sts and working both sides separately, bind off 2 sts from each neck edge twice.

FRONT
Work as for back until armhole measures 8 (8, 8¹/₂, 8¹/₂, 9)"/20.5(20.5, 21.5, 21.5, 23)cm.
Neck shaping
Next row (RS) Work 30 (32, 34, 37, 38) sts, join a 2nd ball of yarn and bind off center 20 (20, 22, 22, 24) sts, work to end. Working both sides at once, bind off 2 sts from each neck edge twice, dec 1 st every other row 2 times. When same length as back, shape shoulder as on back.

SLEEVES
With size 6 (4mm) needles, cast on 47 sts. Beg pat st #1 as foll:
Row 1 (RS) K1, *p3, k4; rep from * end p3, k1. Cont in pat st #1 as established inc 1 st each side every 6th row 14(14, 16, 16, 18) times—75(75, 79, 79, 83) sts. Work even until piece measures 17 1/2"/44.5cm from beg.
Cap shaping
Bind off 8 sts at beg of next 2 rows, 3 sts at beg of next 2 rows, 2 sts at beg of next 2 rows, 1 st at beg of next 4 rows. Bind off rem 45(45, 49, 49, 53) sts.

FINISHING
Block pieces to measurements. Sew left shoulder seam. Pick up and k 76 (76, 80, 80, 84) sts evenly around neck edge. Work in k1, p1 rib for 7 rows. Bind off in rib. Sew right shoulder and neckband seam. Sew sleeves into armholes. Sew side and sleeve seams.
(See schematics on page 134)

Modern Classic

for beginner knitters

Mari Lynn Patrick's buttonless jacket, knit in one piece, offers comfort for days of reflection and relaxation. Add a separate collar and garter stitch edging for subtle accent. "Modern Classic" first appeared in the Winter '98/'99 issue of *Family Circle Easy Knitting* magazine.

MATERIALS

- *Lamb's Pride Bulky* by Brown Sheep, 4oz/113g skeins, each approx 125yd/114m (wool/mohair)
  8 (9, 9, 10, 10, 11) skeins #M23 fuchsia
- One pair size 10.5 (7mm) straight needles
- Size 10.5 (7mm) circular needle, 36"/90cm long
- 2yd/1.85m of 1"/2.5cm grosgrain ribbon and thread to match

SIZES

Sized for Small (Medium, Large, X-Large, XX-Large, XXX-Large). Shown in size Large.

FINISHED MEASUREMENTS

- Bust (closed) 43 (45, 47½, 49½, 52, 54½)"/109 (114, 120.5, 125.5, 132, 138.5)cm
- Length 27¾ (28½, 29¼, 30, 31, 31¼)"/70.5 (72.5, 74.5, 76, 78.5, 79.5)cm
- Upper arm 16 (17, 17½, 19¼, 20, 21)"/40.5 (43, 44.5, 49, 50.5, 53)cm

GAUGE

14 sts and 20 rows to 4"/10cm over St st using larger needle.
TAKE TIME TO CHECK YOUR GAUGE

Note
Cardigan is made all in one piece, beg at lower edge of back and ending at lower edge of fronts.

BACK

With smaller needles cast on 74 (78, 82, 86, 90, 94) sts. K 2 rows for hem. Change to larger circular needle and work back and forth as with straight needles as foll:

Row 1 (RS) Knit.
Row 2 K2 (selvage sts), p to last 2 sts, k2 (selvage sts). Rep these 2 rows until piece measures 19½ (20, 20½, 20½, 21, 21)"/49.5 (50.5, 52, 52, 53, 53) cm from beg, end with a WS row.

Beg sleeves
Cont to work the k2 garter sts in the same place (for armhole detail as in photo), AT SAME TIME, cast on 6 sts at beg of next 14 (18, 20, 4, 0, 0) rows, 5 sts at beg of next 6 (2, 0, 20, 24, 24) rows—188 (196, 202, 210, 210, 214) sts.
Next row (RS) Knit.
Next row (WS) K2 (sleeve cuff trim), [p to sleeve detail, k2] twice, p to last 2 sts, k2 (sleeve cuff trim). Work even on all sts until there are 20 (22, 24, 24, 26, 28) rows in sleeve cuff and sleeve cuff measures 4 (4½, 4¾, 4¾, 5¼, 5½)"/10 (11.5, 12, 12, 13.5, 14)cm. End with a WS row. This completes back and half of sleeves.

Beg left front
Next row (RS) Work 84 (87, 90, 94, 94, 95) sts and sl to a holder to be worked later for right front, bind off center 20 (22, 22, 22, 22, 24) sts for neck and work to end. Work 3 rows even on these 84 (87, 90, 94, 94, 95) sts for left front.
Next row (RS) Inc 1 st at beg of row (neck edge), work to end. Cont to inc 1 st at neck edge every other row 3 times more, then cast on 2 sts at neck edge every other row twice, cast on 3 sts once, cast on 3 (4, 4, 4, 4. 5) sts once—98 (102, 105, 109, 109, 111) sts.
Next row (WS) Work as established to last 4 sts, k4.

Next row (RS) K3, p1 (for front band), work established pat to end. Cont to work in this way until there are a total of 40 (44, 48, 48, 52, 56) rows in sleeve cuff and sleeve cuff measures 8 (9, 9½, 9½, 10½, 11)"/20.5 (23, 24, 24, 26.5, 28)cm, end with a RS row. Corresponding to cast-ons, bind off from sleeve cuff edge, 5 sts 3 (1, 0, 10, 12, 12) times, 6 sts 7 (9, 10, 2, 0, 0) times—41 (43, 45, 47, 49, 51) sts. Cont to work k2 selvage sts and front band detail as before, work even until there are same number of rows as back. Change to smaller needles, k2 rows and bind off.

RIGHT FRONT

Work to correspond to left front, reversing shaping and detail placements.

FINISHING

Block pieces to measurements. Turn lower edges of hems (along ridge) on fronts and back to WS and sew in place. Sew side and sleeve seams.

Collar
Note
Collar is picked up and knit around shaped neck edge in st increments at ends of rows until all sts are picked up to front bands.

(Continued on page 135)

26

Easy Does it

Big Easy
for beginner knitters

A symphony of soft lines, slim shaping, and ample texture makes this ¾-length cardigan an absolute essential for home and office. While set-in sleeves and collar complete the look, the simple pattern of knit and purl stitches make it a project that can be accomplished over a long weekend. The "Big Easy" first appeared in the Fall '97 issue of *Family Circle Easy Knitting* magazine.

MATERIALS

- *Skye* by Colinette/Unique Kolours, 3½oz/100g, each approx 163yd/149m (wool) 10 (10,12) balls in #78 mediterranean
- *Mohair* by Colinette/Unique Kolours, 3½oz/100g, each approx 190yd/ 174m (mohair/wool/nylon) 4 (4, 4) balls in #118 velvet damson
- Size 19 (15mm) circular needle OR SIZE TO OBTAIN GAUGE
- Six 1"/25mm buttons

SIZES

Sized for Small (Medium and Large). Shown in size Medium.

FINISHED MEASUREMENTS

- Bust (buttoned) 47 (51, 55)"/119.5 (129.5, 139.5)cm
- Length 26½ (28, 29)"/67 (71, 73.5)cm
- Width at upper arm 18 (19, 21)"/46 (48, 53.5)cm

GAUGE

8 sts and 10 rows to 4"/10cm in Rib pat using size 19 (15mm) circular needle and 3 strands of yarn held tog.
TAKE TIME TO CHECK GAUGE.

Note

Work with one strand of each yarn held tog throughout.

STITCHES USED

Rib pat (even # of sts)
Row 1 (RS) Knit
Row 2 Purl
Rows 3 and 4 *K1, p1; rep from * to end.
Rows 5 and 6 Rep rows 1 and 2.

Rows 7 and 8 *P1, k1; rep from * to end. Rep rows 1-8 for Rib pat.

BACK

Cast on 44 (48, 52) sts. K 2 rows. Work in Rib pat until piece measures 17½ (18½, 18½)"/44.5 (47, 47)cm from beg, end with a WS row.
Armhole shaping
Bind off 2 sts at beg of next 4 rows—36 (40, 44) sts. Work even until armhole measures 9 (9½, 10½)"/23 (24, 26.5)cm. Bind off all sts.

LEFT FRONT

Cast on 26 (28, 30) sts. K 2 rows. **Next row (RS)** Work in Rib pat to last 2 sts, k2 (for front band). Cont in pat as established, working 2 sts at front edge in garter st (k every row) and rem sts in Rib pat, until piece measures same length as back to underarm. Shape armhole at beg of RS rows as for back—22 (24, 26) sts. Work even until armhole measures 6 (6½, 7½)"/15 (16.5, 19)cm, end with a RS row.
Neck shaping
Next row (WS) Bind off 4 sts (neck edge), work to end. Cont to bind off at neck edge 3 sts

twice, 2 sts once—10 (12, 14) sts. Work even until piece measures same as back to shoulder. Bind off all sts.

RIGHT FRONT

Work to correspond to left front, reversing shaping.

SLEEVES

Cast on 16 (18, 20) sts. K 2 rows. Work in Rib pat, inc 1 st each side (working inc sts into pat) every other row 0 (0, 3) times, every 4th row 10 (10, 8) times—36 (38, 42) sts. Work even until piece measures 19 (19, 18)"/48 (48, 46)cm from beg, end with a WS row.
Cap shaping
Bind off 2 sts at beg of next 4 rows— 28 (30, 34) sts. Bind off all sts.

FINISHING

Block pieces to measurements. Sew shoulder seams.
Collar
With WS facing, pick up and k 15 sts evenly along left front neck edge, 16 sts along back
(Continued on page 136)

Urban Renewal

for intermediate knitters

With a ribbed trim and handy front pockets, Mari Lynn Patrick's uptown belted wrap cardigan in vibrant pumpkin livens up any dull day. Combine two contrasting yarns and knit in stockinette stitch to provide a hip tweedy effect and non-stop versatility. "Urban Renewal" first appeared in the Fall '98 issue of *Family Circle Easy Knitting* magazine.

MATERIALS
- *8 Ply* by Wool Pak Yarns NZ/ Baabajoes Wool Co., 8oz/250g skeins, each approx 525yd/484m (wool)
  3 (3, 4) skeins each in red (A) and orange (B)
- One pair each sizes 8 and 11 (5 and 8mm) needles OR SIZE TO OBTAIN GAUGE
- Size F (4mm) crochet hook
- Stitch holders and markers

SIZES
Sized for Small (Medium, Large, X-Large). Shown in size Medium.

FINISHED MEASUREMENTS
- Bust (closed) 44 (46$^{1}/_{2}$, 48, 51)"/111.5 (118, 122, 129.5)cm
- Length 28$^{1}/_{2}$ (29, 29$^{1}/_{2}$, 30)"/72.5 (74, 75, 76.5)cm
- Upper arm 14 (15, 15$^{1}/_{2}$, 16$^{1}/_{4}$)"/35.5 (38, 39.5, 41)cm

GAUGE
17 sts and 23 rows to 6"/15.25cm over St st using 1 strand A and B held tog and larger needles. TAKE TIME TO CHECK YOUR GAUGE.

Note
Work with one strand A and B held tog throughout.

BACK
With smaller needles and 1 strand each A and B held tog, cast on 64 (68, 70, 74) sts.
Row 1 (RS) K1 (selvage st), *k2, p2; rep from *, end k2 (2, 0, 0), k1 (selvage st). Cont in k2, p2 rib as established for 2"/5cm. Change to larger needles and cont in St st (with k1 selvage sts each side), until piece measures 18$^{1}/_{2}$"/47cm from beg.

Armhole shaping
Row 1 (RS) K2tog 0 (1, 1, 0) time, k to last 2 sts, k2tog 0 (1, 1, 0) time.
Row 2 K1, p to last st, k1.
Row 3 K to last 5 sts, SK2P, k2.
Row 4 K1, p to last 5 sts, p3tog, p1, k1.
Rows 5 and 6 Work even. Rep rows 3-6 for 3 (3, 3, 4) times more—48 (50, 52, 54) sts. Work even until armhole measures 8$^{1}/_{2}$ (9, 9$^{1}/_{2}$, 10)"/21.5 (23, 24, 25.5)cm.

Neck and shoulder shaping
Bind off 5 sts at beg of next 6 (4, 2, 0) rows, 6 sts at beg of next 0 (2, 4, 6) rows. Bind off rem 18 sts for back neck.

LEFT FRONT
With smaller needles and A and B held tog, cast on 38 (40, 41, 43) sts. Work in k2, p2 rib as for back (with selvage sts) for 2"/5cm. Change to larger needles and cont in St st (with k1 selvage sts) until piece measures 17$^{1}/_{2}$ (18, 18$^{1}/_{2}$, 19)"/44.5 (46, 47, 48.5)cm from beg. end with a WS row (On large size, neck shaping will beg $^{1}/_{2}$"/1.25cm above armhole.)

Neck shaping
Next row (RS) Work to last 2 sts, k2tog (neck edge). Cont to dec at neck edge every 4th row 4 times more, every 2nd row twice and place a marker at the last neck dec, AT SAME TIME, when piece measures 18$^{1}/_{2}$"/47cm from beg,

shape armhole as for right side of back. When neck shaping to marker is completed, cont to shape neck by dec 1 st every 2nd row 8 times more—15 (16, 17, 18) sts. When same length as back, shape shoulder as for back.

RIGHT FRONT
Work as for left front, reversing all shaping and matching ribs at center front.

SLEEVES
With smaller needles and A and B held tog, cast on 34 (34, 38, 38) sts. Beg and end with k1 selvage sts, work in k2, p2 rib for 6"/15.5cm, dec 8 (8, 10, 10) sts evenly across last WS row—26 (26, 28, 28) sts. Change to larger needles and cont in St st inc 1 st each side every 4th row 3 (4, 4, 5) times, every 6th row 5 times—42 (44, 46, 48) sts. Work even until piece measures 14"/35.5cm above ribbing or 20"/50.5cm from beg.

Cap shaping
Row 1 (RS) K2tog, k to last 2 sts, k2tog. **Row 2** K1, p to last st, k1. Then rep rows 3-6 of back armhole shaping 4 times, rows 3 and 4 once. Work 0 (0, 0, 2) rows even. Bind off rem 20 (22, 24, 26) sts.

POCKETS
With larger needles and A and B held tog, cast on 22 sts. Work in St st (with k1 selvage sts each

Easy Does it

side) for 4½"/11.5cm, inc 6 sts evenly across last WS row—28 sts. Change to smaller needles. **Row 1 (RS)** K1, *k2, p2; rep from *, end k3. Cont in rib as established for 3"/7.5cm. Bind off in rib.

BELT

With smaller needles and A and B held tog, cast on 10 sts. Work in k1, p1 rib for 60"/152cm. Bind off.

FINISHING

Block pieces to measurements. Sew shoulder seams.

LEFT FRONT LAPEL
Note

The RS rows of the lapel will be the WS when lapel is folded back.

With smaller needles and A and B held tog, cast on 2 sts.

Row 1 (RS) P2.

Row 2 Cast on 2 sts, p2, k2.

Row 3 P2, k2.

Row 4 Cast on 3 sts, work even in rib.

Row 5 Work even in rib. Rep last 2 rows 5 times more—22 sts. After completing last row (row 15), cont to pick up and k sts along straight edge of left front (beg at neck marker) for left front band, picking up 70 (74, 76, 78) sts evenly. Work in k2, p2 rib until band measures 2¾"/7cm. Bind off in rib.

RIGHT FRONT LAPEL

Work to correspond to left front lapel only reverse lapel shaping as foll: Cast on 2 sts.

Row 1 (WS) P2.

Row 2 (RS) Cast on 2 sts, k2, p2. Cont to cast on 3 sts at beg of RS rows a total of 6 times. Work 1 more WS row. Place sts on a holder. Separately, pick up and k sts along center front, then work across 22 sts of lapel.

COLLAR

With smaller needles and A and B held tog, pick up and k 78 sts around neck edge.

Next row K2, *p2, k2; rep from * to end. Cont in k2, p2 rib for 1 row.

Next row (RS) K2, M1 k st, work to last 2 sts, M1 k st, k2. Cont to inc 1 st in this way every 2nd row (working incs into rib pat) 3 times more—86 sts. Work even until collar measures 5"/12.5cm. Bind off in rib. Sew collar to edge of lapel for 13 rows or 2½"/6.5cm. Fold back lapel and steam press lightly.

Belt loops

With crochet hook and A and B held tog, ch 12. Sl st in each ch. Fasten off. Sew belt loops to side seams at 8½"/21.5cm from lower edge. Sew on pockets at top of rib and 3"/7.5cm from center front. Sew sleeves into armholes. Sew side seams. Sew sleeve seams with last 3"/7.5cm on RS for cuff turnback.

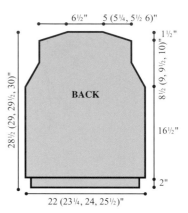

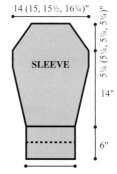

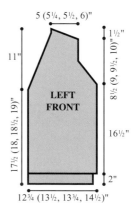

Cool Crochet
for intermediate crocheters

Worked in rich jewel-toned chenille yarn, Melissa Leapman's crochet sweaters will have you celebrating the holiday festivities in refined elegance. The face-framing square neckline, set-in sleeves, and modern openwork "Arch" pattern create the lighter-than-air appearance. "Cool Crochet" first appeared in the Winter '99/'00 issue of *Family Circle Easy Knitting* magazine.

MATERIALS
- *Chenille Sensations* by Lion Brand Yarn Co., 1.4oz/40g skeins, each approx 87yd/80m (100% Acrilan® Acrylic)
  18 (19, 20) skeins in #401 purple multi or #145 violet
- Size H/8 (5mm) crochet hook OR SIZE TO OBTAIN GAUGE

SIZES
Sized for Small (Medium, Large). Shown in size Medium.

FINISHED MEASUREMENTS
- Bust 38 (43, 47½)"/96.5 (109, 120.5)cm
- Length 28 (29, 29)"/71 (73.5, 73.5)cm
- Upper arm 17 (17, 19)"/43 (43, 48)cm

GAUGE
Gauge swatch of 21 sts is 5"/12.5cm wide and 9 rows is 4¼"/11cm long. Ch 23 and work in arch pat st on 21 sts for 9 rows.
TAKE TIME TO CHECK YOUR GAUGE.

ARCH PATTERN STITCH
(ch a multiple of 5 plus 3)
Foundation row (WS) Dc in 4th ch from hook, *ch 3, skip 2 ch, 1 dc in next 3 ch; rep from *, end ch 2, skip next 2 ch, dc in last 2 ch. Ch 1, turn.
Row 1 Sc in first dc, *5 dc in ch-2 sp, skip next dc, sc in next dc; rep from *, end with 5 dc in ch-2 sp, sc in top of turning ch. Ch 5, turn.
Row 2 Skip first sc and first dc, *dc in next 3 dc, ch 2, skip next 3 sts; rep from *, end dc in next 3 dc, ch 1, tr in last sc. Ch 3, turn.
Row 3 Work 2 dc in ch-1 sp, *skip next dc, sc in next dc, 5 dc in next ch-2 sp; rep from *, end skip next dc, sc in next dc, 3 dc into turning ch. Ch 3, turn.

Row 4 Skip first dc, dc in next dc, *ch 2, skip next 3 sts, dc in next 3 dc; rep from *, end ch 2, skip next 3 sts, dc in next dc, dc in top of turning ch. Ch 1 turn. Rep rows 1-4 for arch pat st.

Note
Each dc and each sc count as 1 st, each ch-2 sp counts as 2 sts.

BACK
Ch 83 (93, 103). Work even in arch pat st on 81 (91, 101) sts until piece measures 19½"/49.5cm from beg, end with row 2 of pat.

Armhole shaping
Sl st across first 8 sts, ch 1, sc in next dc, *5 dc in next ch-2 sp, skip next dc, sc in next dc; rep from * to within last 8 sts, leave these sts unworked and ch 5, turn. Cont in arch pat st until armhole measures 8 (8, 9)"/20.5 (20.5, 23)cm, end with pat row 4 (4, 2). Ch 3, turn.

Neck and shoulder shaping
Next row (RS) Dc in next 15 (20, 25) sts, fasten off for first shoulder. Skip center 35 sts and join yarn and ch 3, dc in last 15 (20, 25) sts. Fasten off for second shoulder.

FRONT
Work as for back until armhole measures 5"/12.5cm, end with pat row 2. Ch 3, turn.

Neck shaping
First shoulder work pat st over 15 (20, 25) sts, work to end. Work even in pat until same length as back. On last row, work 15 (20, 25) dc. Fasten off. Skip center 35 sts and work other shoulder to correspond.

SLEEVES
Ch 43 (43, 53). Work even in arch pat st on 41 (41, 51) sts through row 1 of pat. Piece measures approx 1"/2.5cm from beg. Ch 3, turn. Inc row 1 Dc in first sc, ch 2, skip next st, *dc in next 3 dc, ch 2, skip 3 sts; rep from * end with 2 dc in last sc. Ch 1, turn. Inc row 2 Sc in first dc, *5 dc in next ch-2 sp, skip next dc, sc in next dc; rep from *, end with 5 dc in next ch-2 sp, sc in top of t-ch. Ch 5, turn. Inc row 3 Skip first sc and first dc, *dc in next 3 dc, ch 2, skip next 3 sts; rep from *, end with dc in next 3 dc, ch 1, tr in last sc. Ch 3, turn. Inc row 4 Work 2 dc in ch-1 sp, *skip next dc, sc in next dc, 5 dc in ch-2 sp; rep from *, end with skip next dc, sc in next dc, 3 dc in turning ch. Ch 3 turn. Work 2 rows even. Rep last 6 rows 5 times more—71 (71, 81) sts. Work even until piece measures 20½ (19½, 19½)"/52 (49.5, 49.5)cm from beg. For small and large sizes, fasten off. For medium size, ch 3, turn. Skip first st, dc in each st across. Fasten off.

(Continued on page 136)

Tropical Coolers
Ultra-feminine, beachside wearables are the hottest looks under the sun.

Pretty in Pink

for beginner knitters

Designer Mari Lynn Patrick gives a flirty flourish to a classic cardigan with a garter-edging on collar and neckline and delicate picot-edging on the cuffs. Better yet, this sweet luxury knits quick with three strands of yarn held together. "Pretty in Pink" first appeared in the Spring/Summer '99 issue of *Family Circle Easy Knitting* magazine.

MATERIALS

- *Grace* by Patons®, 1³⁄₄oz/50g balls, each approx 136yd/125m (cotton)
  7 (7, 9, 10) balls in #60437 pink
- One pair each size 10.5 and 15 (7 and 10mm) needles OR SIZE TO OBTAIN GAUGE
- Crochet hook size F/5 (4mm)
- Six ³⁄₄"/20mm buttons
- Stitch holders

SIZES

Sized for Small (Medium, Large, X-Large). Shown in size Medium.

FINISHED MEASUREMENTS

- Bust (buttoned) 33 (36, 38, 41)"/83.5 (91.5, 96.5, 104)cm
- Length 19¹⁄₄ (19³⁄₄, 20¹⁄₄, 20³⁄₄)"/49 (50, 51.5, 52.5)cm
- Upper arm 13 (14, 14¹⁄₂, 15¹⁄₄)"/33 (35.5, 37, 39)cm

GAUGE

11 sts and 14 rows to 4"/10cm over St st using 3 strands of yarn and larger needles.
TAKE TIME TO CHECK YOUR GAUGE.

BACK

With smaller needles and 3 strands of yarn, cast on 46 (50, 54, 58) sts.
Row 1 (RS) K2, *p2, k2; rep from * to end.
Row 2 K1 (selvage st), p1, *k2, p2; rep from * end last rep p1, k1 (selvage st). Rep rows 1 and 2 for rib twice more. K next RS rows. Change to larger needles and k next WS row, inc 1 (2, 0, 0) sts—47 (52, 54, 58) sts. Work even in St st (with k1 selvage sts each side of row) until piece measures 11¹⁄₂"/29cm from beg.

Armhole shaping

Bind off 3 sts at beg of next 2 rows.

Next row (RS) K1, SKP, k to last 3 sts, k2tog, k1.
Next row K1, p to last st, k1. Rep last 2 rows 1 (2, 2, 3) times more—37 (40, 42, 44) sts. Work even (with selvage sts) until armhole measures 7 (7¹⁄₂, 8, 8¹⁄₂)"/18 (19, 20.5, 21.5)cm.

Shoulder shaping

Bind off 5 (5, 6, 6) sts at beg of next 2 rows, 5 (6, 6, 6) sts at beg of next 2 rows. Bind off rem 17 (18, 18, 20) sts for back neck.

LEFT FRONT

With smaller needles and 3 strands of yarn, cast on 26 (30, 30, 34) sts. Rep rows 1 and 2 of back 3 times.
Next row (RS) K20 (24, 24, 28) sts inc 2 (0, 2, 0) sts evenly, sl last 6 sts to a holder to be worked later for band—22 (24, 26, 28) sts rem. Change to larger needles and k next WS row. Then cont in St st (with k1 selvage sts each side) until piece measures 11¹⁄₂"/29cm from beg.

Armhole shaping

Next row (RS) Bind off 3 sts, work to end. Work 1 row even.

Next row (RS) K1, SKP, k to end. Work 1 row even. Rep last 2 rows 1 (2, 2, 3) times more—17 (18, 20, 21) sts. Work even until armhole measures 2¹⁄₂ (3, 3¹⁄₂, 4)"/6.5 (7.5, 9, 10)cm.

Neck shaping

Next row (RS) K to last 2 sts, k2tog. Cont to dec 1 st at neck edge every row 4 (4, 5, 8) times more,

every other row 2 (2, 2, 0) times—10 (11, 12, 12) sts rem. Place a yarn marker at neck edge on last dec row. Work even until armhole measures same as back. Shape shoulder as on back.

RIGHT FRONT

Work to correspond to left front, reversing shaping and having 6-st band at beg of RS rows and working one yo, p2tog buttonhole in center of band when piece measures ¹⁄₂"/ 1.25cm from beg.

SLEEVES

With smaller needles and 3 strands of yarn, cast on 22 (22, 22, 26) sts. Work in rib and garter ridge as on back for 2"/5cm changing to larger needles on 2nd row. Then cont in St st, inc 1 st each side every 4th row 8 (9, 10, 9) times—38 (40, 42, 44) sts. Work even in St st until piece measures 17"/43cm from beg.

Cap shaping

Bind off 3 sts at beg of next 2 rows, 2 sts at beg of next 4 rows, dec 1 st each side every other row 4 (5, 6, 7) times—16 sts. Bind off.

FINISHING

Block pieces lightly to measurements. With smaller needles, work in rib across 6 sts of left front band, inc 1 st at inside edges for selvage

(Continued on page 137)

Fringe Benefits

Featuring fashionable ¾-length set-in sleeves, Jean Schafer-Albers's poncho-inspired swing top is stitched in stockinette and saturated in vivid, beach-friendly color. Fringed edges add a fun, whimsical touch. "Fringe Benefits" first appeared in the Spring/Summer '01 issue of *Family Circle Easy Knitting* magazine.

MATERIALS

- *Imagine* by Classic Elite Yarns, 1¾oz/50g balls, each approx 93yds/85m (cotton) 10 (11, 13, 13) balls in #9292 red
- One pair size 6 (4mm) needles OR SIZE TO OBTAIN GAUGE
- Size 5 (3.75mm) circular needle, 16"/40cm long
- Size B/1 (2mm) crochet hook

SIZES

Sized for Small (Medium, Large, X-Large). Shown in size Medium.

FINISHED MEASUREMENTS

- Bust 36 (38, 40½, 42)"/91.5 (96.5, 102.5, 106.5)cm
- Lower width 42 (43½, 45, 46½)"/106.5 (110.5, 114, 118)cm
- Length 26¼ (27, 27½, 28)"/66.5 (68.5, 69.5, 71)cm
- Upper arm 11½ (12, 12½, 13¼)"/29 (30.5, 31.5, 33.5)cm

GAUGE

21 sts and 27 rows to 4"/10cm over St st using size 6 (4mm) needles.
TAKE TIME TO CHECK YOUR GAUGE.

BACK

With straight needles, cast on 2 sts. K 1 row. Cont to work in St st, cast on 2 sts beg of next 54 (56, 58, 60) rows—110 (114, 118, 122) sts. Cont in St st, dec 1 st each side every 6th (6th, 8th, 8th) row 5 (1, 3, 3) times, then every 8th (8th 10th, 10th) row 3 (6, 3, 3) times—94 (100, 106, 110) sts. Work even until piece measures 16¾ (17¼, 17½, 17¾)"/42.5 (43.5, 44.5, 45)cm from beg, end with a WS row.

Armhole shaping

Bind off 8 sts at beg of next 2 rows, dec 1 st each side of next row, then every other row 1 (3, 2, 3) times more—74 (76, 84, 86) sts. Work even until armhole measures 8½ (8¾, 9, 9¼)"/21.5 (22, 23, 23.5)cm.

Shoulder shaping

Bind off 7 (7, 8, 8) sts beg of next 4 (6, 6, 4) rows, 6 (0, 0, 9) sts beg of next 2 (0, 0, 2) rows. Bind off rem 34 (34, 36, 36) for back neck.

FRONT

Work as for back until armhole measures 5¾ (6, 6¼, 6½)"/14.5 (15, 16, 16.5)cm, end with a WS row.

Neck shaping

Next row (RS) Work 29 (30, 34, 35) sts, join 2nd ball of yarn and bind off center 16 sts, work to end. Working both sides at once, bind off from neck edge 3 sts once, 2 sts once, dec 1 st each side every other row 4 (4, 5, 5) times—20 (21, 24, 25) sts. When same length as back to shoulders, shape shoulders as for back.

SLEEVES

Cast on 50 (52, 56, 60) sts. Work in St st, inc 1 st each side every 12th row 1 (1, 3, 3) times, then every 10th row 4 (4, 2, 2) times—60 (62, 66, 70) sts. Work even until piece measures 9½ (9½, 10, 10)"/24 (24, 25.5, 25.5)cm from beg, end with a WS row.

Cap shaping

Bind off 8 sts at beg of next 2 rows, dec 1 st each side of next row, then every other row 1 (3, 2, 3) times, every 6th row 4 (5, 3, 1) times, every 4th row 2 (0, 4, 7) times. Bind off 2 (2, 3, 3) sts at beg of next 4 rows. Bind off rem 20 (20, 18, 18) sts.

FINISHING

Block pieces to measurements. Sew shoulders. With RS facing and circular needle, pick up and k 34 (34, 36, 36) sts across back neck edge, 22 (22, 23, 23) sts along each side of neck edge and 16 sts along front neck edge—94 (94, 98, 98) sts. Join and work in k1, p1 rib for 1½"/3cm. Bind off all sts in pat. Set in sleeves. Sew side and sleeve seams. Cut fringe 5"/12.5cm long. On wrong side of bottom edge and sleeve edge, insert crochet hook from front to back through piece and over folded yarn. Pull yarn through. Draw ends through and tighten. Trim yarn.

(See schematics on page 137)

Cream of the Crop

for beginner knitters

A cropped boxy pullover, designed by Rosemary Drysdale, knits in a flash with three strands of lightweight cotton yarn held together. A boatneck and slight shaping add the perfect finishing touch. "Cream of the Crop" first appeared in the Spring/ Summer '99 issue of *Family Circle Easy Knitting* magazine.

MATERIALS
- *Goa* by GGH/Muench Yarns, 1¾oz/50g balls, each approx 66yd/ 60m (cotton) 25 (29, 31, 33, 37) balls in #113 blue
- One pair size 15 (10mm) needles OR SIZE TO OBTAIN GAUGE
- Size J/10 (6mm) crochet hook
- Stitch markers

SIZES
Sized for Small (Medium, Large, X-Large, XX-Large). Shown in size Medium.

FINISHED MEASUREMENTS
- Bust 40 (43, 46, 49, 52)"/101.5 (109, 117, 124.5, 132)cm
- Length 17 (17½, 18, 19, 19½)"/43 (44.5, 45.5, 48.5, 49.5)cm
- Upper arm 17 (18, 19, 20, 21)"/43 (45.5, 48, 50.5, 53)cm

GAUGE
8 sts and 12 rows to 4"/10cm over St st using size 15 (10mm) needles and 3 strands of yarn held tog.
TAKE TIME TO CHECK YOUR GAUGE.

Notes
1 Work with three strands of yarn held tog throughout.
2 K first and last st of every row for garter st selvage. These sts are not counted in the finished measurements.

BACK
With 3 strands of yarn held tog, cast on 42 (45, 48, 51, 54) sts. Work in St st and garter st selvages until piece measures 16 (16½, 17, 18, 18½)"/40.5 (42, 43, 46, 47)cm from beg, end with a WS row.

Neck shaping
Next row (RS) Work 15 (16, 17, 18, 20) sts, join a 2nd ball of yarn and bind off center 12 (13, 14, 15, 14) sts, work to end. Working both sides at once, bind off 2 sts from each neck edge once. Work even, if necessary, until piece measures 17 (17½, 18, 19, 19½)"/43 (44.5, 45.5, 48.5, 49.5)cm from beg. Bind off rem 13 (14, 15, 16, 18) sts each side for shoulders.

FRONT
Work as for back until piece measures 15 (15½, 16, 17, 17½)"/38 (39.5, 40.5, 43.5, 44.5)cm from beg, end with a WS row.

Neck shaping
Next row (RS) Work 16 (17, 18, 19, 21) sts, join a 2nd ball of yarn and bind off center 10 (11, 12, 13, 12) sts, work to end. Working both sides at once, bind off from each neck edge 2 sts once, 1 st once. Work even until piece measures same as back. Bind off rem 13 (14, 15, 16, 18) sts each side for shoulders.

SLEEVES
With 3 strands of yarn held tog, cast on 18 (18, 18, 20, 20) sts. Work in St st, inc 1 st each side every 4th row 3 (5, 8, 7, 10) times, every 6th row 6 (5, 3, 4, 2) times—36 (38, 40, 42, 44) sts. Work even until piece measures 17½ (18, 18, 18½, 18½)"/44.5 (45.5, 45.5, 47, 47)cm from beg. Bind off.

FINISHING
Block pieces to measurements. Sew shoulder seams. Place markers 8½ (9, 9½, 10, 10½)"/21.5 (23, 24, 25.5, 26.5)cm down from shoulders on front and back. Sew top of sleeves between markers. Sew side and sleeve seams. With RS facing, crochet hook and 3 strands of yarn held tog, work 1 row of sc evenly around neck. Fasten off.

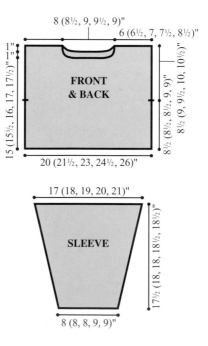

8 (8½, 9, 9½, 9)"
6 (6½, 7, 7½, 8½)"
1"
1"
FRONT & BACK
15 (15½, 16, 17, 17½)"
8½ (9, 9½, 10, 10½)"
8½ (8½, 8½, 9, 9)"
20 (21½, 23, 24½, 26)"

17 (18, 19, 20, 21)"
SLEEVE
17½ (18, 18, 18½, 18½)"
8 (8, 8, 9, 9)"

White Hot

for intermediate knitters

Trimmed with tropical-colored beads along the hem, cuffs and hood, a crisp white hooded cardigan with ¾-length sleeves is a lighthearted must-have for any wayfaring adventure. Attach beads while knitting by using a crochet hook to pull a stitch through each. Designed by Shirley Paden, the "White Hot" cardigan first appeared in the Spring/Summer '00 issue of *Family Circle Easy Knitting* magazine.

MATERIALS

- *Cotton Twist* by Berroco Inc., 1¾oz/50g balls, each approx 85yd/78m (cotton/rayon) 14 (15, 16) balls in #8301 white
- One pair size 7 (4.5mm) needles OR SIZE TO OBTAIN GAUGE
- Sizes B/1 and G/6 (2 and 4.5mm) crochet hooks
- Wooden beads, 8mm, 10mm and 12mm, each in assorted colors. Our sample uses mustard, orange, red, and fuchsia.

SIZES

Sized for Small (Medium, Large). Shown in size Medium.

FINISHED MEASUREMENTS

- Bust (closed) 38 (41, 44)"/96.5 (104, 111.5)cm
- Length 17½ (18, 18½)"/44.5 (46, 47)cm
- Upper arm 17 (18, 19)"/43 (45.5, 48)cm

GAUGE

22 sts and 28 rows to 4"/10cm over St st using size 7 (4.5mm) needles.
TAKE TIME TO CHECK YOUR GAUGE.

Note

Place beads as desired, using photo for inspiration.

BEAD STITCH

On a RS row, k to st immediately below the bead position. K this st wrapping yarn twice around needle. On the next row, p to the st with the double yo, sl st off needle, insert smaller crochet hook into hole of a bead and through dropped st, pull the lp through the bead. Place lp back on LH needle and p it.

BEAD PLACEMENT

Lower edge of body and sleeves

Row 1 (RS) *K2, work bead st, k1; rep from *.

Work 2nd row of bead st.
Row 3 K4, *work bead st, k3; rep from *. Work 2nd row of bead st.
Row 5 Rep row 1. Work 2nd row of bead st. bead placement

Left front edge of hood

Row 1 (RS) Work to last 7 sts, work bead st, k3, work bead st, k2. Work 2nd row of bead st.
Row 3 Work to last 5 sts, work bead st, k4. Work 2nd row of bead st.
Rep these 4 rows.

Right front edge of hood

Row 1 (RS) K4, work bead st, work to end. Work 2nd row of bead st.
Row 3 K2, work bead st, k3, work bead st, work to end. Work 2nd row of bead st.
Rep these 4 rows.

BACK

Cast on 105 (113, 121) sts. P 1 row on WS. Work 6 rows bead placement, then cont in St st until piece measures 9"/23cm from beg.

Armhole shaping

Bind off 3 sts at beg of next 2 rows, 2 sts at beg of next 2 rows, 1 st at beg of next 4 rows—91 (99, 107) sts. Work even until armhole measures 8½ (9, 9½)"/21.5 (23, 24)cm. Bind off all sts.

LEFT FRONT

Cast on 53 (57, 61) sts. P 1 row on WS. Work 6

rows bead placement, then cont in St st until same length as back to armhole. Work armhole decs at beg of RS rows as for back—46 (50, 54) sts. Work even until armhole measures 8½ (9, 9½)"/21.5 (23, 24)cm, end with a WS row. Bind off 26 (30, 34) sts at beg of next RS row for shoulder, work to end—20 sts. Work 1 row even.

Hood

Cast on 42 sts at beg of next RS row, work to end—62 sts. Work even in St st, working bead placement for left front hood, for 8"/20.5cm more, end with a WS row.

Top shaping

Cont bead placement, dec 1 st at beg of next RS row and rep dec at same edge every 4th row 3 times more, every other row twice, bind off 2 sts 6 times, 3 sts 3 times—35 sts. Bind off.

RIGHT FRONT

Work to correspond to left front, reversing all shaping and working bead placement for right front hood.

SLEEVES

Cast on 57 (61, 65) sts. P 1 row on WS. Work 6 rows bead placement, then cont in St st, inc 1 st each side every 4th row 16 (17, 18) times, every 6th row twice—93 (99, 105) sts. Work

(Continued on page 137)

Seashell Cardigan

for intermediate knitters

Intarsia sand dollars and starfish in sun-kissed colors of red, pink, and yellow brighten up a long, lean button-down cardigan. Designed by Wendy Sacks, patch pockets, fold-up cuffs, contrasting embroidery, and striped seed stitch act as artful accents. The "Seashell Cardigan" first appeared in the Spring/Summer '01 issue of *Family Circle Easy Knitting* magazine.

MATERIALS

- *Provence* by Classic Elite Yarns, 4oz/125g balls, each approx 256yds/233m (cotton)
  6 (7) balls in #2601 white (MC)
  1 ball each in #2634 magenta (A), #2630 fuchsia (B), #2658 red (C), #2625 peach (D), #2633 yellow (E)
- One pair each sizes 5, 6 and 7 (3.75, 4 and 4.5mm) needles OR SIZE TO OBTAIN GAUGE
- Size 6 (4mm) circular needle, 29"/74cm long
- Size F/5 (4 mm) crochet hook
- Stitch markers
- Four 1½"/38mm buttons
- Bobbins

SIZES

Sized for Small/Medium (Large/X-Large). Shown in size Large.

FINISHED MEASUREMENTS

- Chest 48 (52)"/122 (132)cm
- Length 26 (27)"/66 (68.5)cm
- Upper arm 18 (20)"/45.5 (50.5)cm

GAUGE

19 sts and 24 rows to 4"/10cm over St st using larger needles.
TAKE TIME TO CHECK YOUR GAUGE.

SEED STITCH

Row 1 K1, *p1, k1; rep from * to end.
Row 2 K the purl sts and p the knit sts.
Rep row 2 for seed st.

notes

1 When changing colors, twist yarns tog on WS to prevent holes in work. Use a separate bobbin of yarn for each block of color.
2 Sleeves are worked from top down.

BACK

With smaller needles and A, cast on 105 (115) sts. Work in seed st for 2 rows, then work 2 rows each in colors B, C, D and E. Change to larger needles and MC. Work in seed st, inc 8 sts evenly spaced across—113 (123) sts. Cont in St st until piece measures 25 (26)"/63.5 (66)cm from beg.

Shoulder shaping

Bind off 9 (10) sts at beg of next 2 (4) rows, 8 (9) sts at beg of next 6 (4) rows—47 sts. Bind off rem sts for back neck.

LEFT FRONT

With smaller needles and A, cast on 51 (55) sts. Work seed st stripes as for back. Change to larger needles and MC. Work in seed st, inc 4 (5) sts evenly across—55 (60) sts. Cont in St st until piece measures 15 (15½)"/38 (39.5)cm from beg.

Beg chart 1

Beg and end as indicated, work in chart pat, working dec for neck and shoulder shaping as indicated.

RIGHT FRONT

Work same as left front, reversing chart pat and shaping.

RIGHT POCKET

With larger needles and MC, cast on 45 sts. Work in seed st for 3 rows. Change to St st and work even for 4 rows.

Beg chart 2

Work through 42 rows of chart. Work even in St st for 6 rows, change to seed st and work even for 8 rows. With size 5 (3.75mm) needle, bind off firmly.

LEFT POCKET

With larger needles and MC, cast on 45 sts. Work in seed st for 3 rows. Cont in St st for 47 rows, work seed st for 8 rows. With size 5 (3.75mm) needle, bind off firmly.

SLEEVES

Sew shoulder seams. Place markers 9 (10)"/23 (25.5)cm down from shoulders on front and back for shoulders. With RS facing, larger needles and MC, pick up and k 87 (95) sts between markers. Work in St st for 4 rows.

Next row (RS) Dec 1 st each end of this row, then every 5 rows 16 (12) times, every 0 (4) rows 6 times—55 (59) sts. Work even until sleeve measures 15½"/39.5cm, ending with a WS row.

Cuff

Cuff will be turned back, so RS and WS are now reversed. **Next row** Purl, and inc 4 sts evenly spaced across row—59 (63) sts. Next row Knit. **Next row** Purl.

Beg chart 3

Cont in chart for 30 rows. With size 5 (3.75mm) needle, bind off 67 (71) sts firmly.

FINISHING

Block pieces to measurements. Work running st embroidery around all motifs in contrasting colors. Sew pockets to fronts, ½"/1.5cm from side seam edge. Sew side and sleeve seams, reversing seaming at cuffs. Turn cuffs back and tack in place. With crochet hook and MC, work one row of sl st through both layers at bottom of cuffs.

Button band

With RS facing, smaller needle and E, pick up 156 (161) sts from left center back to lower left front edge. Work 2 rows seed st. Cont in seed st working 2 rows each in D, C, B and A. With size 5 (3.75mm) needle, bind off firmly. Place markers on for 4 buttons, the first one ¼"/.5cm from lower edge, the last one just below beg of neck shaping and the other 2 spaced evenly between.

Buttonhole band

With E, pick up sts as for buttonband. Work seed st and stripes as for buttonband, working buttonholes opposite markers on color C stripe as foll: bind off 5 sts for each buttonhole, then cast on 5 sts over bound-off sts on foll row. Bind off firmly.

Sew band tog at center back neck.

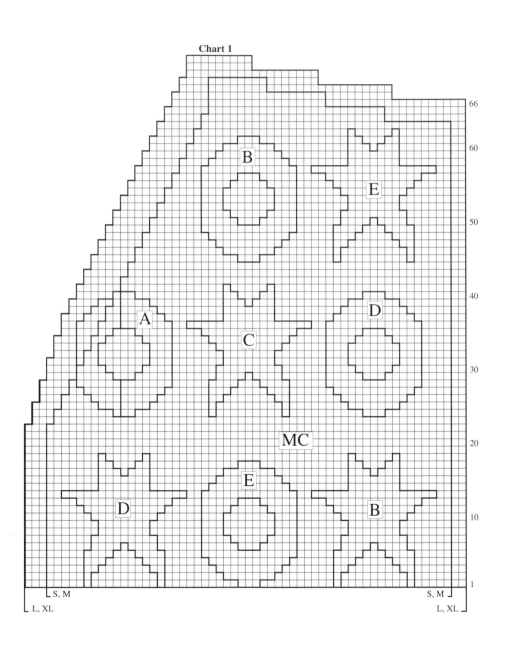

Chart 1

Color Key

White (MC)
Magenta (A)
Fuchsia (B)
Red (C)
Peach (D)
Yellow (E)

Stitch Key

☐ K on RS, p on WS
⊟ P on RS, k on WS

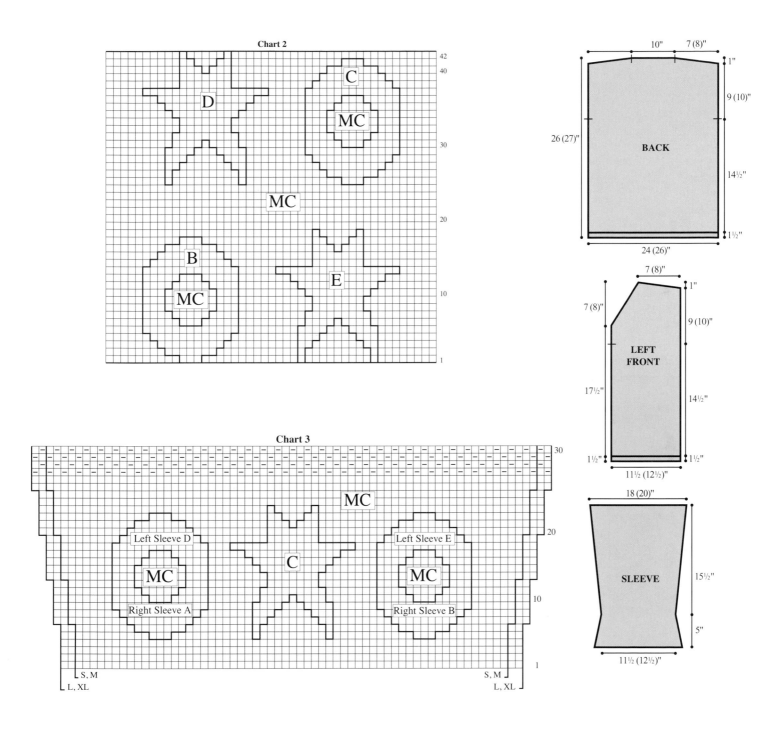

Chart 2

42
40

D

C

MC

30

MC

20

B

MC

E

10

1

Chart 3

30

MC

Left Sleeve D

20

C

MC

MC

Left Sleeve E

Right Sleeve A

10

MC

Right Sleeve B

1

S, M

L, XL

S, M

L, XL

BACK

10"   7 (8)"
1"
9 (10)"
26 (27)"
14½"
1½"
24 (26)"

LEFT FRONT

7 (8)"
1"
7 (8)"
9 (10)"
17½"
14½"
1½"
1½"
11½ (12½)"

SLEEVE

18 (20)"
15½"
5"
11½ (12½)"

Family Values

Great new looks that work for each member of the family.

Maternal Instincts
for beginner knitters

Like mother, like daughters–Laura Gebhardt's timeless trio transcends generations. The teen style is sleeveless while the other two feature bell sleeves and all three are rich in texture, big on comfort. Each is quick to knit in reverse stockinette stitch and features a ribbed turtleneck and edges. "Maternal Instincts" first appeared in the Fall '01 issue of *Family Circle Easy Knitting* magazine.

MATERIALS
Child's version
- *Commotion* by Classic Elite Yarns, 1³⁄₄oz/50g balls, each approx 200yd/184m (wool/nylon)
  4 (5, 6, 6) balls in #4202 opal
Women's version
  9 (10, 10, 11) balls in #4257 blue
Teen's version
  4 (4, 5) balls in #4281 green
- Size I/9 (5.5mm) crochet hook
All versions
- One pair size 10 (6mm) needles OR SIZE TO OBTAIN GAUGE
- Stitch holders

CHILD'S VERSION

SIZES
Sized for Child's 4 (6, 8, 10). Shown in Child's size 4.

FINISHED MEASUREMENTS
- Chest 27 (28¹⁄₂, 29¹⁄₂, 31)"/68.5 (72.5, 75, 78.5)cm
- Length 13¹⁄₂ (14¹⁄₂, 16, 17¹⁄₂)"/34 (37, 40.5, 44.5)cm
- Upper arm 10¹⁄₄ (10¹⁄₄, 11, 12)"/26 (26, 28, 30.5)cm

GAUGE
20 sts and 30 rows to 6"/15cm over reverse St st using double strand of yarn and size 10 (6mm) needles.
TAKE TIME TO CHECK YOUR GAUGE.

Note
Work with two strands of yarn held tog throughout.

BACK
With double strand of yarn, cast on 45 (47, 49, 51) sts. Work in k1, p1 rib for 4 rows. Then, cont in reverse St st until piece measures 7 (8, 9, 10)"/18 (20.5, 23, 25.5)cm from beg.

Armhole shaping
Bind off 3 sts at beg of next 2 rows. Dec 1 st each side every other row twice—35 (37, 39, 41) sts. Work even until armhole measures 5¹⁄₂ (5¹⁄₂, 6, 6¹⁄₂)"/14 (14, 15, 16.5)cm.

Neck and shoulder shaping
Bind off 3 (4, 4, 3) sts at beg of next 2 rows, 3 (3, 3, 4) sts at beg of next 4 rows. Sl rem 17 (17, 19, 19) sts to a holder for back neck.

FRONT
Work as for back until armhole measures 4 (4, 4¹⁄₂, 5)"/10 (10, 11.5, 12.5)cm.

Neck shaping
Next row (RS) Work 13 (14, 14, 15) sts, join 2nd balls of yarn and bind off center 9 (9, 11, 11) sts, work to end. Working both sides at once, dec 1 st each side of neck edge every other row 4

times, AT SAME TIME, shape shoulders when same length as back.

SLEEVES
With double strand of yarn, cast on 30 (30, 34, 38) sts. Work in reverse St st, dec 1 st each side every 6th (6th, 4th, 4th) row 3 (3, 4, 4) times— 24 (24, 26, 30) sts. Work even for 5 rows. Inc 1 st each side of next row then every 8th (8th, 10th, 10th) row twice more, every 12th row twice — 34 (34, 36, 40) sts. Work even until piece measures 15¹⁄₂ (16, 17, 18)"/39.5 (40.5, 43, 45.5)cm from beg.

Cap shaping
Bind off 3 sts at beg of next 2 rows. Dec 1 st each side every other row 9 (9, 10, 11) times. Bind off rem 10 (10, 10, 12) sts.

FINISHING
Block pieces to measurements. Sew one shoulder seam.

Turtleneck
With double strand of yarn, pick up and k 52

(52, 56, 56) sts evenly around neck edge. Work in k1, p1 rib for 8"/20.5cm. Bind off very loosely in rib. Sew other shoulder and turtleneck seam sewing top half from RS for collar turnback. Sew side seams and sleeve seams.

WOMEN'S VERSION

FINISHED MEASUREMENTS
■ Bust 37 (40$\frac{1}{2}$, 44, 47)"/94 (103, 111.5, 119)cm
■ Length 22$\frac{1}{2}$ (23, 24, 25)"/57 (58.5, 61, 63.5)cm
■ Upper arm 15 (15$\frac{1}{2}$, 16$\frac{1}{4}$, 17$\frac{1}{2}$)"/38 (39.5, 41, 44.5)cm

GAUGE
20 sts and 30 rows to 6"/15cm over reverse St st using double strand of yarn and size 10 (6mm) needles.
TAKE TIME TO CHECK YOUR GAUGE.

Note
Work with two strands of yarn held tog throughout.

BACK
With double strand of yarn, cast on 61 (67, 73, 79) sts. Work in k1, p1 rib for 4 rows. Then, cont in reverse St st until piece measures 14 (14, 14$\frac{1}{2}$, 15)"/35.5 (35.5, 37, 38)cm from beg.

Armhole shaping
Bind off 4 (4, 4, 5) sts at beg of next 2 rows. Dec 1 st each side every other row 3 (4, 5, 5) times—47 (51, 55, 59) sts. Work even until armhole measures 7$\frac{1}{2}$ (8, 8$\frac{1}{2}$, 9)"/19 (20.5, 21.5, 23)cm.

Neck and shoulder shaping
Bind off 3 (4, 4, 5) sts at beg of next 4 rows, 4 (4, 5, 5) sts at beg of next 2 rows. Sl rem 27 (27, 29, 29) sts to a holder for back neck.

FRONT
Work as for back until armhole measures 4$\frac{1}{2}$ (5, 5$\frac{1}{2}$, 6)"/11.5 (12.5, 14, 15)cm.

Neck shaping
Next row (RS) Work 16 (18, 19, 21) sts, join 2nd balls of yarn and bind off center 15 (15, 17, 17) sts, work to end. Working both sides at once, dec 1 st from each neck edge every other row 6 times, AT SAME TIME, shape shoulders when same length as back.

SLEEVES
With double strand of yarn, cast on 50 (50, 54, 54) sts. Work in reverse St st dec 1 st each side every 4th row 7 times—36 (36, 40, 40) sts. Work even for 9 rows. Inc 1 st each side of next row and every 10th row 6 (7, 6, 8) times more—50 (52, 54, 58) sts. Work even until piece measures 23 (23$\frac{1}{2}$, 24, 24)"/58.5 (59.5, 61, 61)cm from beg.

Cap shaping
Bind off 4 (4, 4, 5) sts at beg of next 2 rows. Dec 1 st each side every other row 9 (8, 9, 8) times. Bind off 2 sts at beg of next 6 (8, 8, 10) rows. Bind off rem 12 sts.

FINISHING
Block pieces to measurements. Sew one shoulder seam.

Turtleneck
With double strand of yarn, pick up and k 66 (66, 70, 70) sts evenly around neck edge. Work in k1, p1 rib for 10"/25.5cm. Bind off very loosely in rib. Sew other shoulder and turtleneck seam, sewing top half from RS for collar turnback. Sew sleeves into armholes. Sew side and sleeve seams.

TEEN'S VERSION

FINISHED MEASUREMENTS
■ Bust 32 (34, 37)"/81 (86, 94)cm
■ Length 19$\frac{1}{2}$ (20, 20$\frac{1}{2}$)"/49.5 (51, 52)cm

GAUGE
20 sts and 30 rows to 6"/15cm over reverse St st using double strand of yarn and size 10 (6mm) needles.
TAKE TIME TO CHECK YOUR GAUGE.

Note
Work with two strands of yarn held tog throughout.

BACK
With double strand of yarn, cast on 53 (57, 61) sts. Work in k1, p1 rib for 4 rows. Then cont in reverse St st until piece measures 12"/30.5cm from beg.

Armhole shaping
Bind off 3 (3, 4) sts at beg of next 2 rows. Dec 1 st each side every other row 2 (3, 3) times— 43 (45, 47) sts. Work even until armhole measures 6$\frac{1}{2}$ (7, 7$\frac{1}{2}$)"/16.5 (18, 19)cm.

Neck and shoulder shaping
Bind off 4 sts at beg of next 4 (6, 4) rows, 3 (0, 5) sts at beg of next 2 rows. Sl rem 21 sts to a holder for back neck.

FRONT
Work as for back until armhole measures 4$\frac{1}{2}$ (5, 5$\frac{1}{2}$)"/11.5 (12.5, 14)cm.

Neck shaping
Next row (RS) Work 16 (17, 18) sts, join 2nd balls of yarn and bind off center 11 sts, work to end. Working both sides at once, dec 1 st from each neck edge every other row 5 times, AT SAME TIME, shape shoulders when same length as back.

FINISHING
Block pieces to measurements. Sew one shoulder seam.

Turtleneck
With double strand of yarn, pick up and k 56 sts evenly around neck edge. Work in k1, p1 rib for 10"/25.5cm. Bind off very loosely in rib. Sew other shoulder and turtleneck seam sewing top half from RS for collar turnback. Sew side seams. With crochet hook and double strand of yarn, sl st loosely around each armhole edge evenly.

CHILD'S VERSION

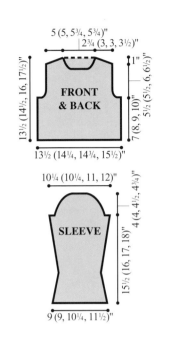

5 (5, 5¾, 5¾)"

2¾ (3, 3, 3½)"

1"

FRONT & BACK

13½ (14½, 16, 17½)"

5½ (5½, 6, 6½)"

7 (8, 9, 10)"

13½ (14¼, 14¾, 15½)"

10¼ (10¼, 11, 12)"

4 (4, 4½, 4¾)"

SLEEVE

15½ (16, 17, 18)"

9 (9, 10¼, 11½)"

WOMEN'S VERSION

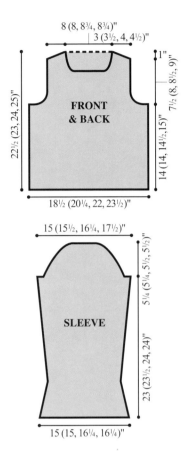

8 (8, 8¾, 8¾)"

3 (3½, 4, 4½)"

1"

FRONT & BACK

22½ (23, 24, 25)"

7½ (8, 8½, 9)"

14 (14, 14½, 15)"

18½ (20¼, 22, 23½)"

15 (15½, 16¼, 17½)"

5¼ (5¼, 5½, 5½)"

SLEEVE

23 (23½, 24, 24)"

15 (15, 16¼, 16¼)"

TEEN'S VERSION

6½" 3¼ (3½, 4)"

1"

FRONT & BACK

19½ (20, 20½)"

6½ (7, 7½)"

12"

16 (17, 18½)"

Seaside Savvy

for beginner knitters

Whether you're spending mornings by the sea or nights by the fireplace, Susan Mills variegated rainbow pullovers—his with a wide neck and hers with a V-neck—combine style with comfort for the ultimate in sweater ease. "Seaside Savvy" first appeared in the Fall '00 issue of *Family Circle Easy Knitting* magazine.

MATERIALS

Women's version

- *Lite-Lopi* by Reynolds/JCA, 1¾oz/50g balls, each approx 109yd/100m (wool)

  1 (2, 2, 2, 3) balls in #432 grape heather (A), 3 (3, 4, 4, 4) balls in #419 ocean (B)

  3 (3, 3, 4, 4) balls in #418 blue heather (C), 2 (3, 3, 3, 4) balls in #422 sage heather (D)

  1 (2, 2, 2, 3) balls in #421 celery heather (E), 1 ball in #420 gold heather (F)

- One pair size 10 (6mm) needles OR SIZE TO OBTAIN GAUGE

Men's version

  2 (2, 3, 3, 4) balls in #432 grape heather (A), 4 (4, 5, 5, 6) balls in #419 ocean (B)

  4 (4, 4, 5, 5) balls in #418 blue heather (C), 3 (3, 4, 4, 4) balls in #422 sage heather (D)

  2 (2, 2, 2, 3) balls in #421 celery heather (E), 1 ball in #426 gold heather (F)

- One pair each sizes 8 and 10 (5 and 6mm) needles OR SIZE TO OBTAIN GAUGE

- Size 8 (5mm) circular needle, 16"/40cm long

SIZES

Women's Version

Sized for Small (Medium, Large, X-Large, XX-Large). Shown in size Medium.

Men's Version

Sized for Men's Small (Medium, Large, X-Large, XX-Large). Shown in size Large.

WOMEN'S VERSION

FINISHED MEASUREMENTS

- Bust 36 (40, 44, 48, 52)"/91.5 (101.5, 111.5, 122, 132)cm

- Length 21 (22, 22, 23, 24)"/53.5 (55.5, 55.5, 58.5, 61)cm

- Upper arm 18 (19½, 19½, 20, 20)"/46 (49, 49, 51, 51)cm

GAUGE

12 sts and 18 rows to 4"/10cm over St st using 2 strands of yarn held tog and size 10 (6mm) needles.

TAKE TIME TO CHECK YOUR GAUGE.

STRIPE PATTERN

Working with 2 strands of yarn, work *2 rows with D and E, 2 rows with E and F, 2 rows with D and E, 4 rows with C and D, 4 rows with B and C, 6 rows with A and B, 4 rows with B and C, 4 rows with C and D; rep from * (28 rows) for stripe pat.

BACK

With 1 strand each D and E, cast on 54 (60, 66, 72, 78) sts. Work in St st and stripe pat until piece measures 20 (21, 21, 22, 23)"/51 (53, 53, 56, 58.5)cm from beg.

Neck and shoulder shaping

Bind off 7 (9, 9, 11, 12) sts at beg of next 2 rows, 8 (9, 10, 11, 13) sts at beg of next 2 rows, AT SAME TIME, bind off center 22 (22, 26, 26, 26) sts and working both sides at once, dec 1 st from each neck edge once.

FRONT

Work as for back until piece measures 13 (14, 13½, 14, 15)"/33 (35.5, 34, 35.5, 38)cm from beg.

V-neck shaping

Next row (RS) Work 27 (30, 33, 36, 39) sts, join another 2 strands of yarn and work to end. Working both sides at once, work 1 row even.

Dec row (RS) Work to last 4 sts on first side, k2tog, k2; on second side, k2, ssk, work to end. Rep dec row every other row 10 (10, 12, 11, 11) times more, every 4th row 1 (1, 1, 2, 2) times— 15 (18, 19, 22, 25) sts rem each side. When same length as back, shape shoulders as on back.

SLEEVES

With 1 strand each D and E, cast on 30 sts. Work in St st and stripe pat, inc 1 st each side every 4th row 0 (2, 2, 8, 8) times, every 6th row 10 (12, 12, 7, 7) times, every 8th row 2 (0, 0, 0, 0) times—54 (58, 58, 60, 60) sts. Work even until piece measures 21 (21, 21, 20, 20)"/53 (53, 53, 51, 51)cm from beg. Bind off.

FINISHING

Block pieces to measurements. Sew shoulder seams. Place markers at 9 (9¾, 9¾, 10, 10)"/23

(24.5, 24.5, 25.5, 25.5)cm down from shoulders. Sew sleeves to armholes between markers. Sew side and sleeve seams.

MEN'S VERSION

FINISHED MEASUREMENTS
■ Chest 40 (44, 48, 52, 56)"/101.5 (111.5, 122, 132, 142)cm
■ Length 24$\frac{1}{2}$ (24$\frac{1}{2}$, 25$\frac{1}{2}$, 25$\frac{1}{2}$, 26$\frac{1}{2}$)"/62 (62, 65, 65, 67)cm
■ Upper arm 20 (20, 21$\frac{1}{2}$, 21$\frac{1}{2}$, 22)"/51 (51, 54, 54, 56)cm

GAUGE
12 sts and 18 rows to 4"/10cm over St st using 2 strands of yarn held tog and larger needles. TAKE TIME TO CHECK YOUR GAUGE.

Note
Work with two strands of yarn held tog throughout.

STRIPE PATTERN
Working with 2 strands of yarn, work *4 rows with B and C, 4 rows with C and D, 2 rows with D and E, 2 rows with E and F, 2 rows with D and E, 4 rows with C and D, 4 rows with B and C, 6 rows with A and B; rep from * (28 rows) for stripe pat.

BACK
With smaller needles and 1 strand A and B, cast on 60 (66, 72, 78, 84) sts.

Row 1 (RS) *P1, k1 tbl; rep from * to end.
Row 2 *P1 tbl, k1; rep from * to end. Rep these 2 rows for twisted rib for 2$\frac{1}{2}$"/6.5cm. Change to larger needles, and cont in St st and stripe pat until piece measures 23$\frac{1}{2}$ (23$\frac{1}{2}$, 24$\frac{1}{2}$, 24$\frac{1}{2}$, 25$\frac{1}{2}$)"/59.5 (59.5, 62, 62, 65)cm from beg.

Neck and shoulder shaping
Next row (RS) Work 20 (23, 25, 28, 30) sts, join another 2 strands of yarn and bind off center 20 (20, 22, 22, 24) sts, work to end. Working both sides at once, bind off 1 st from each neck edge twice. Bind off rem 18 (21, 23, 26, 28) sts each side for shoulders.

FRONT
Work as for back until piece measures 22$\frac{1}{2}$ (22$\frac{1}{2}$, 23$\frac{1}{2}$, 23$\frac{1}{2}$, 24$\frac{1}{2}$)"/57 (57, 59.5, 59.5, 62)cm from beg.

Neck shaping
Next row (RS) Work 23 (26, 28, 31, 33) sts, join another 2 strands of yarn and bind off center 14 (14, 16, 16, 18) sts, work to end. Working both sides at once, bind off 2 sts from each neck edge twice, 1 st once—18 (21, 23, 26, 28) sts rem each side for shoulders. When same length as back, bind off rem sts each side for shoulders.

SLEEVES
With smaller needles and 1 strand each A and B, cast on 30 (30, 32, 32, 34) sts. Work in k1, p1 twisted rib for 2$\frac{1}{2}$"/6.5cm. Change to larger needles and cont in St st and stripe pat, inc 1 st

each side every 4th row 8 (8, 9, 9, 9) times, every 6th row 7 times—60 (60, 64, 64, 66) sts. Work even until piece measures 22$\frac{1}{2}$"/57cm from beg. Bind off.

FINISHING
Block pieces to measurements. Sew shoulder seams.

Neckband
With circular needle and 1 strand each A and B, pick up and k 66 (66, 68, 68, 68) sts evenly around neck edge. Join.
Rnd 1 *K1 tbl, p1; rep from * around. Rep rnd 1 for twisted rib for 1$\frac{1}{4}$"/3cm. Bind off. Place markers at 10 (10, 10$\frac{3}{4}$, 10$\frac{3}{4}$, 11)"/25.5 (25.5, 27, 27, 28)cm down from shoulders. Sew sleeves to armholes between markers. Sew side and sleeve seams.

WOMEN'S VERSION

MEN'S VERSION

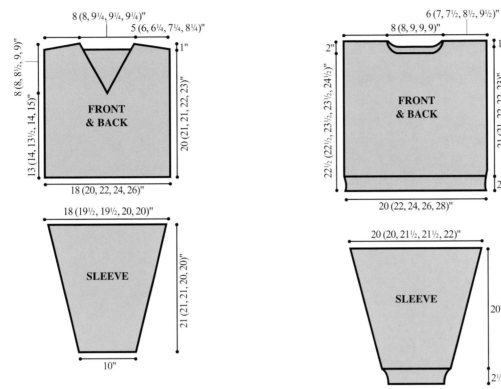

WOMEN'S VERSION

8 (8, 9¼, 9¼, 9¼)"

5 (6, 6¼, 7¼, 8¼)"

1"

8 (8, 8½, 9, 9)"

20 (21, 21, 22, 23)"

FRONT & BACK

13 (14, 13½, 14, 15)"

18 (20, 22, 24, 26)"

18 (19½, 19½, 20, 20)"

SLEEVE

21 (21, 21, 20, 20)"

10"

MEN'S VERSION

6 (7, 7½, 8½, 9½)"

8 (8, 9, 9, 9)"

2"

1"

21 (21, 22, 23)"

22½ (22½, 23½, 23½, 24½)"

FRONT & BACK

2½"

20 (22, 24, 26, 28)"

20 (20, 21½, 21½, 22)"

SLEEVE

20"

2½"

10 (10, 10½, 10½, 11¼)"

Family Affair

for beginner knitters

When it comes to brilliant colors and chunky textures, Mom knows best. Knit with two strands at a time, these zip-front pullovers designed by Barbara Khouri have ribbed collars, moss-stitch yokes, and adorable animal pulls. They're wonderful wearables for every member of the family. "Family Affair" appeared first in the Fall '99 issue of *Family Circle Easy Knitting* magazine.

MATERIALS

Child's version
- *Dover* by Reynolds/JCA, 1¾oz/50g balls each approx 82yd/75m (wool)
  10 (11, 13, 15) balls in #25 denim or #22 red
- Size 11 (8mm) circular needle, 16"/40cm long
- Neck zipper 5"/12.5cm long

Women's version
- 21 (22, 24, 26, 27) balls in #21 med purple
- Size 11 (8mm) circular needle, 24"/60cm long
- Neck zipper, 6"/15cm long

Both versions
- One pair each sizes 11 and 13 (8 and 9mm) needles OR SIZE TO OBTAIN GAUGE
- Size K/10½ (7mm) crochet hook
- Decorative zipper pull provided by Trendsetter Yarns

SIZES

Child's version
Sized for Child's 2 (4, 6, 8). Shown in size 4.
Women's version
Sized for Small (Medium, Large, X-Large, XX-Large). Shown in size Medium.

CHILD'S VERSION

FINISHED MEASUREMENTS
- Chest 28 (32, 36, 38)"/71 (81, 91, 96.5)cm
- Length 15¾(16¾, 17¾, 19¾)"/40 (42.5, 45, 50)cm
- Upper arm 13 (14, 15, 16)"/33 (35.5, 38, 41)cm

GAUGE
10 sts and 13 rows to 4"/10cm over St st using a double strand of yarn and larger needles. TAKE TIME TO CHECK YOUR GAUGE.

Notes
1 Work with two strands of yarn held tog throughout.
2 Due to the seaming for this extra bulky style, finished measurements reflect sewn pieces, not exact schematic pieces.

BACK
With smaller needles and a double strand of yarn, cast on 38 (42, 46, 50) sts. Beg with a p row, work in St st for 3 rows (end of rolled edge). Change to larger needles and cont in St st until piece measures 6½ (7, 7½, 9)"/16.5 (18, 19, 23)cm from beg with edge rolled, end with a RS row.

Beg ridge pat
Row 1 (WS) Knit.
Rows 2 and 3 Purl.
Row 4 *K2, p2; rep from * end k2. Row 5 *P2, k2; rep from *, end p2.
Rows 6 and 7 Rep rows 4 and 5.
Rows 8 and 9 Knit.
Rows 10 and 11 Purl.

Beg moss st
Rows 1 and 2 *K1, p1; rep from * to end. **Rows 3 and 4** *P1, k1; rep from * to end. Rep rows 1-4 for moss st until piece measures 5½ (6, 6½, 7)"/14 (15, 16.5, 18)cm from beg of moss st pat.

Neck shaping
Work 15 (16, 18, 20) sts, join another double strand of yarn and bind off center 8 (10, 10, 10)

sts, work to end. Working both sides at once, bind off 3 sts from each neck edge once. On next RS row, bind off rem 12 (13, 15, 17) sts each side for shoulders.

FRONT
Work as for back until 11 rows of ridge pat are completed. Work 0 (0, 0, 2) more rows in moss st.

Beg placket opening
Next row (RS) Work 19 (21, 23, 25) sts, join another double strand of yarn and work in pat to end. Work both sides at once until placket opening measures 5"/12.5cm, end with a WS row.

Neck shaping
Next row (RS) Work first side, bind off 4 sts at beg of row on 2nd side, work to end. Rep last row once more. Then bind off 2 sts from each neck edge once, dec 1 st every other row 1 (2, 2, 2) times. When same length as back, bind off rem 12 (13, 15, 17) sts each side for shoulders.

SLEEVES
With smaller needles and a double strand of

yarn, cast on 22 (22, 26, 26) sts. Beg with a WS row, work 11 rows in ridge pat as on back. Change to larger needles and St st, inc 1 st each side every other row 6 (6, 3, 4) times, every 4th row 2 (3, 5, 5) times—38 (40, 42, 44) sts. Work even until piece measures 10 (11, 11½, 12)"/25.5 (28, 29, 30.5)cm from beg with edge rolled. Bind off.

FINISHING
Block pieces to measurements. Sew shoulder seams.

COLLAR
With circular needle and a double strand of yarn, pick up and k 50 (54, 54, 54) sts evenly around neck edge. Beg and end with k2, work in k2, p2 rib for 4"/10cm. Bind off in rib. With crochet hook and a double strand of yarn, work an edge of sc around placket opening. Sew zipper into placket. With center of top of sleeves at shoulder seams, sew sleeves into armholes along moss st section. Sew side and sleeve seams. Attach zipper pull to zipper, if desired.

WOMEN'S VERSION

FINISHED MEASUREMENTS
■ Bust 45 (48, 51, 54, 57)"/114 (122, 129.5, 137, 144.5)cm
■ Length 25¼ (25¾, 26¼, 26¾, 27¼)"/64 (65.5, 66.5, 68, 69)cm
■ Upper arm 17½ (18½, 19½, 20½, 21)"/44.5 (47, 49.5, 52, 53.5)cm

GAUGE
10 sts and 13 rows to 4"/10cm over St st using a double strand of yarn and larger needles.
TAKE TIME TO CHECK YOUR GAUGE.

Notes
1 Work with two strands of yarn held tog throughout.
2 Due to the seaming for this extra bulky style, finished measurements reflect sewn pieces, not exact schematic pieces.

BACK
With smaller needles and a double strand of yarn, cast on 58 (62, 66, 70, 74) sts. Beg with a p row, work in St st for 3 rows (end of rolled edge). Change to larger needles and cont in St st as established until piece measures 14"/35.5cm from beg with edge rolled, end with a RS row.
Beg ridge pat
Row 1 (WS) Knit.
Rows 2 and 3 Purl.
Row 4 *K2, p2; rep from *, end k2.
Row 5 *P2, k2; rep from *, end p2.
Rows 6 and 7 Rep rows 4 and 5.
Rows 8 and 9 Knit.
Rows 10 and 11 Purl.
Beg moss st
Rows 1 and 2 *K1, p1; rep from * to end.
Rows 3 and 4 *P1, k1; rep from * to end. Rep rows 1-4 for moss st until piece measures 7½ (8, 8½, 9, 9½)"/19 (20.5, 21.5, 23, 24)cm from beg of moss st pat.
Neck shaping

Next row (RS) Work 23 (25, 27, 28, 30) sts, join another double strand of yarn and bind off center 12 (12, 12, 14, 14) sts, work to end. Working both sides at once, bind off 3 sts from each neck edge once. On next RS row, bind off rem 20 (22, 24, 25, 27) sts each side for shoulders.

FRONT
Work as for back until 11 rows of ridge pat are completed. Work 0 (0, 2, 4, 4) more rows in moss st.
Beg placket opening
Next row (RS) Work 29 (31, 33, 35, 37) sts, join another double strand of yarn and work in pat to end. Work both sides at once until placket opening measures 6"/15cm, end with a WS row.
Neck shaping
Next row (RS) Work first side, bind off 4 sts at beg of row on 2nd side, work to end. Rep last row once more. Then bind off 3 (3, 3, 4, 4) sts from each neck edge once, dec 1 st every other row twice. When same length as back, bind off rem 20 (22, 24, 25, 27) sts each side for shoulders.

SLEEVES
With smaller needles and a double strand of yarn, cast on 28 (30, 30, 32, 32) sts. Beg with a WS row, work 11 rows in ridge pat as on back. Change to larger needles and cont in St st, inc 1 st each side of next row then every 4th row 9 (9, 10, 10, 11) times more—48 (50, 52, 54, 56) sts. Work even until piece measures 17 (17, 17½, 17½, 18)"/43 (43, 44.5, 44.5, 45.5)cm from beg. Bind off.

FINISHING

Block pieces to measurements. Sew shoulder seams.

COLLAR

With circular needle and a double strand of yarn, pick up and k 66 (66, 66, 70, 70) sts evenly around neck edge. Beg and end with k2, work in k2, p2 rib for 5"/12.5cm. Bind off in rib. With crochet hook and a double strand of yarn, work an edge of sc around placket opening. Sew zipper into placket. With center of top of sleeve at shoulder seams, sew sleeves into armholes along moss st section. Sew side and sleeve seams. Attach zipper pull to zipper, if desired.

WOMEN'S VERSION

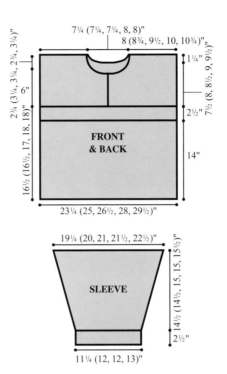

CHILD'S VERSION

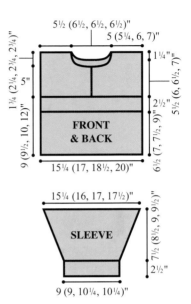

Outdoor Gear

for beginner knitters

Pack a family weekend outdoors with lots of fun and easy to knit, rugged rugby sweaters designed by Mari Lynn Patrick. Dad wears a zippered crewneck with rugby stripes while Mom's cardigan features optional tartan ribbon button bands. The boy's cross pullover has a striped yoke and cross stitch pattern that knits in a flash. "Outdoor Gear" first appeared in the Fall '95 issue of *Family Circle Easy Knitting* magazine.

MATERIALS

Men's sweater

- *Shetland Ragg Chunky* by Patons®, 3¹⁄₂oz/100g balls, each approx 161yd/147m (acrylic/wool)
  9 (10, 10, 11) balls in #701 stone (MC)
- *Shetland Chunky* by Patons®, 3¹⁄₂oz/50g balls, each approx 80yd/75m
  1 ball each in #2320 navy (A) and #2118 gray (B)
- One pair each sizes 9 and 10¹⁄₂ (5¹⁄₂ and 7 mm) needles OR SIZE TO OBTAIN GAUGE
- Size 9 (5¹⁄₂ mm) circular needle 16"/40cm long
- 5"/12.5cm heavy metal zipper in navy
- Sewing needle and thread to match zipper

Women's sweater

- *Shetland Ragg* by Patons®, 3¹⁄₂oz/100g, each approx 161yds/145m (acrylic/wool)
  6 (6, 7, 8) balls in #716 hickory
- One pair each sizes 9 and 10 (5¹⁄₂ and 6mm) needles OR SIZE TO OBTAIN GAUGE
- Seven ³⁄₄"/20mm buttons
- Stitch holders and markers
- 1¹⁄₂ yd/1.5m of 1³⁄₈"/4cm plaid ribbon and matching sewing thread (optional)

SIZES

Men's sweater

Sized for men and women Small (Medium, Large, X-Large). Shown in Medium.

Women's sweater

Sized for Small (Medium, Large, X-Large). Shown in size Medium.

MEN'S SWEATER

KNITTED MEASUREMENTS

- Chest/Bust 44¹⁄₂ (48, 51¹⁄₂, 54)"/113 (122, 131, 137) cm
- Length 24¹⁄₂ (25, 26, 26¹⁄₂)"/62 (63.5, 66, 67.5)cm
- Width at upper arm 18³⁄₄ (20, 21, 21³⁄₄")/47.5 (50.5, 53, 55.5) cm

GAUGE

14 sts and 20 rows to 4"/10cm in St st using size 10¹⁄₂ (7 mm) needles.
TAKE TIME TO CHECK YOUR GAUGE.

STITCHES USED

K2, P2 Rib

(multiple of 4 sts plus 2 extra)

Row 1 (RS) K2, *p2, k2; rep from * to end.

Row 2 K the knit sts and p the purl sts.

Rep rows 1 and 2 for k2, p2 rib.

SKP

Sl 1, k1, psso

SPP

Sl 1, p1, psso

SK2P

Sl 1, k2tog, psso

SP2P

Sl 1, p2tog, psso

BACK

With smaller needles and A, cast on 78 (86, 90, 94) sts and work in k2, p2 rib for 2 rows. Change to MC and work in rib for 4 rows. Change to B and work in rib for 3 rows. Cut A and B. Change to MC and larger needles. **Next Row (WS)** Purl, dec 0 (2, 0, 0) sts evenly spaced—78 (84, 90, 94) sts. Cont in St st (k on RS, p on WS) until piece measures 15 (15, 15¹⁄₂, 15¹⁄₂)"/38 (38, 39.5, 39.5) cm from beg, end with a WS row.

Armhole Shaping

Next row (RS) K to last 4 sts, SKP, k2.

Next row (WS) P to last 4 sts, SPP, p2. Rep last 2 rows 4 times more—68 (74, 80, 84) sts. Work even until armhole measures 9¹⁄₂ (10, 10 ¹⁄₂, 11)"/24 (25.5, 26.5, 28) cm. Bind off all sts.

FRONT

Work as for back until armhole measures 4½ (5, 5½,6)"/11.5 (12.5, 14, 15) cm, end with a WS row.

Neck Shaping

Next row (RS) K27 (30, 32, 34), join 2nd ball of MC and bind off center 14 (14, 16, 16) sts, k to end. Working both sides at once, work 1 row even.

Row 1 (RS) first half: Knit across; second half: K2, SK2P, k to end.

Row 2 (WS) first half: Purl across; second half: P2, SP2P, p to end.

Row 3 (RS) first half: Knit across; second half: K2, SKP, k to end.

Row 4 (WS) first half: Purl across; second half: P2, SPP, p to end. Rep rows 3 and 4 six times more—18 (21, 23, 25) sts each side for shoulders. Work even until same length as back to shoulders. Bind off.

SLEEVES

With smaller needles and A, cast on 34 (34, 34, 38) sts. Work in k2, p2 rib for 2 rows. Change to MC and work in rib for 4 rows. Change to B and work in rib for 4 rows. Change to A and cont in rib until piece measures 5"/12.5 cm from beg, end with a RS row. Cut A and B. Change to MC and larger needles.

Next Row (WS) Purl, inc 0 (2, 2, 0) sts evenly spaced—34 (36, 36, 38) sts. Cont in St st as foll: For women's sizes only: inc 1 st each side every 4th row 14 (17, 15, 16) times, then every 6th (0, 2nd, 2nd) row 2 (0, 4, 3) times—66(70, 74, 76) sts. Work even until piece measures 19¾ (20, 20, 20½)"/50 (51, 51, 52) cm from beg. For men's sizes only: inc 1 st each side every 4th row 6 (9, 15, 14) times then every 6th row 10 (8, 4, 5) times—66 (70, 74, 76) sts. Work even until piece measures 22¾ (23, 23, 23½)"/58 (58.5, 58.5, 59.5) cm from beg.

Cap Shaping

For all sizes: Work same as back armhole shaping. Bind off rem 56 (60, 64, 66) sts.

FINISHING

Block pieces to measurements. Sew shoulder seams.

With RS facing, circular needle and MC, beg at center front neck, pick up and k 96(96, 100, 100) sts evenly around neck. Do not join but work back and forth in rows.

Row 1 (WS) K1, *p2, k2; rep from * end p2 k1.

Row 2 (RS) K1, *k2, p2; rep from * end k3. Rep last 2 rows for rib, working 5 more rows with MC, then 4 rows A, 4 rows MC, 4 rows B, 3 rows A. Bind off in rib. Set in sleeves. Sew side and sleeve seams. Using thread, sew zipper inside neck opening.

WOMEN'S SWEATER

FINISHED MEASUREMENTS

■ Bust (buttoned) 41½ (44, 46¼, 48)"/105.5 (111.5, 117.5, 122)cm

■ Length 21 (21½, 22, 22½)"/53.5 (54.5, 56, 57)cm

■ Width at upper arm 16½ (17¾, 17¾, 18¾)"/42 (45, 45, 47.5)cm

GAUGE

14 sts and 20 rows to 4"/10cm in St st using size 10 (6mm) needles. TO SAVE TIME, TAKE TIME TO CHECK YOUR GAUGE.

STITCHES USED

K1, P1 Rib

(over an odd number of sts)

Row 1 (RS) *K1, p1; rep from *, end k1.

Row 2 P1, *k1, p1; rep from * to end.

Rep rows 1 and 2 for k1, p1 rib.

K2, P2 Rib

(multiple of 4 sts plus 2 extra)

Row 1 (RS) *K2, p2; rep from *, end k2.

Row 2 P2, *k2, p2; rep from * to end.

Rep rows 1 and 2 for k2, p2 rib.

St st

K on RS, p on WS.

SKP

Sl 1, k1, psso.

SK2P

Sl 1, k2tog, pass the k2tog over.

BACK

With smaller needles, cast on 78 (82, 86, 90) sts. Work in k2, p2 rib for 2"/5cm. Change to larger needles. P next row on WS, dec 4 (3, 3, 4) sts evenly across—74 (79, 83, 86) sts. Cont in St st until piece measures 12 (12, 12½, 12½)"/30.5 (30.5, 31.5, 31.5)cm from beg, end with a WS row.

Armhole shaping

Next Row (RS) K2, SK2P, work to last 5 sts, k3tog, k2. P 1 row. Rep last 2 rows twice more.

Next Row (RS) K2, SKP, work to last 4 sts, k2tog, k2. P 1 row. Rep last 2 rows once more—58 (63,67,70) sts. Work even until armhole measures 8 (8½, 8½, 9)"/20.5 (21.5, 21.5, 23)cm, end with a WS row.

Shoulder and neck shaping

Bind off 5 (0, 7, 7) sts at beg of next 4 (0, 4, 6) rows, 6 sts at beg of next 2 (6, 2, 0) rows, AT SAME TIME, bind off center 14 (15, 15, 16) sts for neck and working both sides at once, bind off from each neck edge 3 sts twice.

LEFT FRONT

With smaller needles, cast on 40 (44, 44, 48) sts.

Next Row (RS) Work in k2, p2 rib over 34 (38, 38, 42) sts, beg with a p1, work k1, p1 rib over last 6 sts. Cont in rib as est for 2"/5cm. Change to larger needles. Cont as foll: **Next row (WS)** Rib 6 sts and place on a holder, p to end, dec 0 (2, 0, 2) sts evenly across—34 (36, 38, 40) sts. Cont in St st until same length as back to armhole. Shape armhole at side edge (beg of RS rows) as for back—26 (28, 30, 32) sts. Work even until armhole measures 7 (7½, 7½, 8)"/18 (19, 19, 20.5)cm, end with a RS row.

Neck shaping

Next row (WS) Bind off 3 (3, 3, 4) sts (neck

edge), work to end. Cont to bind off from neck edge 3 sts once more, 2 sts once, then dec 1 st at same edge every other row twice, AT SAME TIME, when same length as back to shoulder, shape shoulder at side edge as for back. With smaller needles, work across 6 rib sts for band and cont in k1, p1 rib until band fits along center front to neck. Place sts on a holder. If not using ribbon at front edge, place markers on band for 6 buttons, the first one at ¾"/2cm from lower edge, the last on at 2½"/6.5cm from top, the others spaced evenly between.

RIGHT FRONT

Work to correspond to left front, reversing shaping. If not using ribbon at front edge, work buttonholes opposite markers as foll: on a RS row, rib 2, k2tog, yo, work to end.

SLEEVES

With smaller needles, cast on 30 (34, 34, 34) sts. Work in k2, p2 rib for 2½"/6.5cm. Change to larger needles. Cont in St st, inc 1 st each side every 4th row 7 (5, 4, 8) times, every 6th row 7 (9, 10, 8) times—58 (62, 62, 66) sts. Work even until piece measures 18¼ (18½, 19, 19½)"/46.5 (47, 48.5, 49.5)cm from beg, end with a WS row.

Shape cap

Work as for back armhole shaping. Bind off rem 42 (46, 46, 50) sts.

FINISHING

Block pieces to measurements. Sew shoulder seams.

Front bands

Sew bands to fronts, adjusting length if necessary.

Neckband

With RS facing and smaller needles, beg at right front neck, rib across sts of holder, pick up and k 66 (66, 66, 70) sts evenly around neck edge, rib across sts on left front neck holder—78 (78, 78, 82) sts. Keeping first and last 6 sts in k1, p1 rib, work rem 66 sts in k2, p2 rib for 1 row. If not using ribbon band, work a buttonhole on right front edge as before. Cont in rib until neckband measures 1½"/4cm. Bind off in rib. If using ribbon band, work as foll: Leaving 1 st at front edge free, sew ribbon to front with sewing thread. Sew 7 buttons on left front band, the first on at ¾"/2cm from lower edge, the last one at ¾"/2cm from top, the others spaced evenly between. On right front, oposite buttons, make hand-stitched buttonholes. Set in sleeves. Sew side and sleeve seams. Sew on buttons.

MEN'S SWEATER

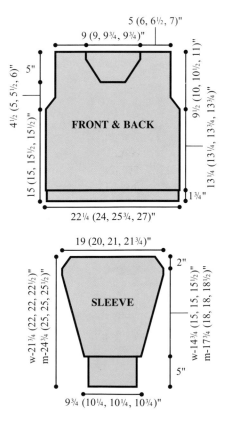

WOMEN'S SWEATER

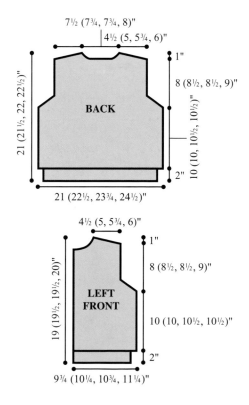

MATERIALS

Child's sweater

- *Candide* by Reynolds, 3¹/₂oz/100g balls, each approx 170 yd/153m (wool) (3, 4, 4, 5)/[6, 6, 7, 7] balls in #102 oatmeal (MC), (1);[2] balls each of #4 navy (A) and #6 ecru (B)
- One pair each sizes 7 and 10 (4¹/₂ and 6 mm) needles OR SIZE TO OBTAIN GAUGE.

Hat

- *Shetland Chunky* by Patons®, 3¹/₂oz/100g, balls, each approx 161yd/147m (acrylic/wool)
  2 balls in #2232 (MC)
- *Shetland Chunky Ragg* by Patons®, 3¹/₂oz/100g, each approx 80 yd/75m (acrylic/wool)
  1 ball each in #7035 navy (A) and #7029 seafoam (B)
- One set (4) dpn size 9 (5¹/₂mm) OR SIZE TO OBTAIN GAUGE
- Stitch markers

SIZES

Child's sweater

Sized for children's sizes (6, 8, 10, 12) women or men [Small, Medium, Large, Extra-Large]. Shown in children's size 8.

Hat

One size fits all.

FINISHED MEASUREMENTS

- Chest/Bust (35, 37, 39, 41) [43, 45, 47, 49]"/(89, 94, 99, 104) [109, 114, 119, 124] cm
- Length (17¹/₂, 18¹/₂, 20¹/₂, 22) [25, 25¹/₂, 26¹/₂, 27]"/(44.5, 47, 52, 56) [63.5, 65, 67, 68.5] cm
- Width at upper arm (14¹/₂, 15¹/₄, 16, 17¹/₂) [18, 19¹/₂, 20¹/₄, 21¹/₂]"/(37, 39, 40.5, 44.5) [45.5, 49.5, 51.5, 54.5] cm

GAUGES

- 17 sts and 22 rows to 4"/10cm in crossed pat st using size 9 (5¹/₂ mm) needles.
- 15 sts and 22 rows to 4"/10cm in St st using size 9 (5¹/₂ mm) needles.

TAKE TIME TO CHECK YOUR GAUGES.

CROSSED PATTERN RIB

(multiple of 3 sts plus 1)

Row 1 (RS) K1, *sl 1 purlwise, k1, pass sl st over the k1 and put it on LH needle and k it tbl, p1; rep from * end last rep k1 instead of p1.

Row 2 K1, *p2, k1; rep from * to end.

Rep these 2 rows for crossed pat rib.

CROSSED PATTERN ST

(multiple of 3 sts plus 1)

Row 1 (RS) *K1, sl 1 purlwise, k1, pass sl st over the k1 and put it on LH needle and k it tbl; rep from * end k1.

Row 2 K1, p to last st, k1. Rep these 2 rows for crossed pat st.

STRIPE PAT

Work in St st (k on RS, p on WS) as foll: *2 rows A, 2 rows; rep from * (4 rows) for stripe pat.

Note

For easier working, circle all the numbers that pertain to your size.

BACK

With smaller needles and MC, cast on (76, 82, 85, 88) [94, 97, 103, 106)] sts. Work in crossed pat rib for (1³/₄) [2¹/₂]"/(4.5) [6.5]cm, end with a RS row. Change to larger needles and work row 2 of crossed pat st. Cont in crossed pat st until piece measures (9¹/₂, 10, 11¹/₂, 12¹/₂)/[15, 15, 15¹/₂, 15¹/₂]"/(24, 25.5, 29, 32) [38, 38, 39.5, 39.5] cm from beg, end with a RS row.

Beg Yoke

Next Row (WS) With A, k1 then purl across dec (9, 10, 10, 10) [11, 11, 12, 12] sts evenly, end k1—(67, 72, 75, 78)[83, 86, 91, 94] sts.

Dec Row 1 (RS) Cont stripe pat, work to last 5 sts, SKP, K3.

Dec Row 2 K1, Work to last 5 sts, p2tog, p2, k1. Cont stripe pat, rep last 2 rows (5)[5] times more—(55, 60, 63, 66) [71, 74, 79, 82] sts. Work even in stripe pat until armhole measures (6³/₄, 7¹/₄, 7³/₄, 8¹/₄) [8³/₄, 9¹/₄, 9³/₄, 10¹/₄]"/17, 18.5, 19.5, 21) [22, 23.5, 25, 26] cm, end with a RS row.

Neck and Shoulder Shaping

Next Row (WS) Work (21, 23, 24, 25) [27, 28, 30, 31] sts, join 2nd ball of yarn and bind off center (13, 14, 15, 16) [17, 18, 19, 20] sts, work to end. Working both sides at once, bind off 3 sts from each neck edge twice and AT SAME TIME, beg shoulder shaping on next row, binding off from each shoulder edge (5, 6, 6, 6,) [7, 7, 8, 8] sts 3(2, 3, 2) [3, 2, 3, 2] times, (0, 5, 0, 7) [0, 8, 0, 9] sts once.

FRONT

Work as for back until armhole measures (4³/₄, 5¹/₄, 5³/₄, 6¹/₄) [6¹/₄, 6³/₄, 7¹/₄, 7³/₄]"/12, 13.5, 14.5, 16) [16, 17, 18.5, 19.5] cm, end with a RS row.

Neck Shaping

Next Row (WS) Bind off center (13, 14, 15, 16) [17, 18, 19, 20] sts as for back.

Next Row (RS) Working both sides at once,

work left side of neck as foll: K to last 4 sts, SKP, k2; work right side of neck as foll: K to end.

Next Row (WS) Right side of neck: Work to last 4 sts, p2tog, p1, k1; left side of neck: work to end. Rep these 2 rows for neck dec 5 times more (15, 17, 18, 19) [21, 22, 24, 25] sts rem each side. Work even until armhole measures (7, 7½, 8, 8½) [9, 9½, 10, 10½]"/(18, 19,20.5,21.5) [23, 24, 25.5, 26.5] cm. Work shoulder shaping as for back.

SLEEVES
Note
Sleeve length for women's and men's styles are different as noted in instructions.

With smaller needles and MC, cast on (34, 31, 34, 34) [37, 37, 40, 40] sts. Work in crossed rib pat for (1¾) [2½]"/(4.5) [6.5] cm, end with a RS row. Change to larger needles and work row 2 of crossed pat st. Cont in crossed pat st inc 1 st each side (working incs inside of k selvage sts and into pat), as foll:

For children: every 2nd row (5, 10, 5, 7) times, every 4th row (10, 8, 13, 14) times—(64, 67, 70, 76) sts. Work even until piece measures (11¼, 12, 13¾, 15¼)"/(28.5, 30.5, 35, 39) cm from beg.

For women: every 2nd row [6, 10, 10, 13] times, every 4th row [15, 14, 14, 14] times—[79, 85, 88, 94] sts. Work even until piece measures [16½, 17¼, 17½, 18¼]"/[42, 44, 44.5, 46.5] cm from beg. For men: every 2nd row [0, 4, 4, 8] times, every 4th row [21, 20, 20, 19] times—[79, 85, 88, 94] sts. Work even until piece measures [18½, 19¼, 19½, 20¼]/[47, 49, 49.5, 51.5] cm from beg.

Cap Shaping
For all sizes: Rep dec rows 1 and 2 of back armhole 3 times—(58, 61, 64, 70) [73, 79, 82, 88] sts.
Next Row (RS) K3, k2tog, pat to last 5 sts SKP, k3.
Next Row (WS) K1, p2, p2togtbl, p to last 5 sts, p2tog, p2, k1. Rep these 2 rows 3 times more (42, 45, 48, 54) [57, 63, 66, 72] sts. Bind off.

FINISHING
Block pieces. Sew right shoulder seam. With smaller needles and MC, pick up and k (70, 73, 73, 76) [85, 88, 91, 94] sts evenly around neck. Work in crossed pat rib for (1) [1½]"/(2.5)[4] cm. Bind off in rib pat on RS row. Sew left shoulder and neckband seam. Set sleeves into armhole. Sew side and sleeve seams.

HAT
GAUGE
22 sts and 22 rows to 4"/10cm in k1, p1 rib (unstretched) using size 9 (5.5mm) needles. TAKE TIME TO CHECK YOUR GAUGE.

CUFF
With size 9 dpn and A, cast on 80 sts. Divide sts evenly over 3 needles (26 sts on first and last needles, 28 sts on middle needle). Join and place marker for beg of rnd. Work in k1, p1 rib as foll: 2 rnds A, 4 rnds MC, 3 rnds B. Cont in rib with MC only until piece measures 10"/25.5cm from beg.

Crown shaping
Next rnd Knit.
Next rnd [K4, k2tog] 13 times, k2tog—66 sts.
Next rnd [K4, k2tog] 11 times—55 sts.
Next rnd [K3, k2tog] 11 times—44 sts.
Next rnd [K2, k2tog] 11 times—33 sts.
Next rnd [K1, k2tog] 11 times—22 sts.
Next rnd [K2tog] 11 times—11 sts.
Cut yarn. Thread through rem sts on needle. Pull tog tightly and secure. Fold back lower edge to RS to form cuff.

CHILD'S SWEATER

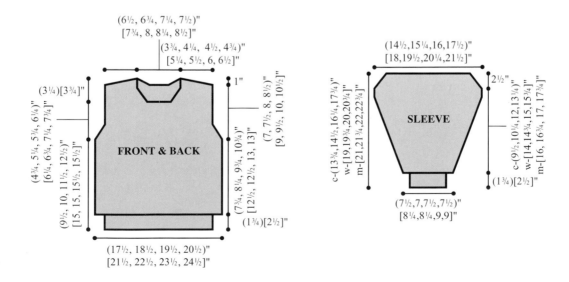

Natural Beauty
for intermediate knitters

Tricia McKenzie's his-and-hers pullovers are destined to become weekend staples. Her cream-colored, placket-front pullover complements his classic gray-toned crew. Both have raglan-sleeves and ribbed edges and wear well with everything. "Natural Beauty" first appeared in the Fall '99 issue of *Family Circle Easy Knitting* magazine.

MATERIALS
Women's version
- ■ *8 Ply* by Wool Pak Yarns NZ/Baabajoes Wool Co., 7¼oz/250g hanks, each approx 525yd/472m (wool)
  4 (4, 5) hanks in natural
- ■ Sizes 3 and 5 (3 and 3.75mm) circular needles, 16"/40cm long
- ■ Stitch holders

Men's version
- 4 (5, 5) hanks in tussock
- ■ Size 3 (3mm) circular needle, 16"/40cm long

Both versions
- ■ One pair each sizes 3 and 5 (3 and 3.75mm) needles OR SIZE TO OBTAIN GAUGE

SIZES
Women's version
Sized for Small (Medium, Large). Shown in size Medium.

Men's version
Sized for Men's Small (Medium, Large). Shown in size Large.

WOMEN'S VERSION

FINISHED MEASUREMENTS
- ■ Bust 44 (48, 53)"/111.5 (122, 134.5)cm
- ■ Length 25½ (26½, 27¼)"/64.5 (67, 69)cm
- ■ Upper arm 17 (17¾, 18½)"/43 (45, 47) cm

GAUGE
21 sts and 38 rows to 4"/10cm over pat st using larger needles.
TAKE TIME TO CHECK YOUR GAUGE.

PATTERN STITCH
(multiple of 4 sts plus 3 see chart)

Note
Foll written instructions or chart for pat st.
Row 1 (RS) K3, *p1, k3; rep from * to end.
Row 2 K1, *p1, k3; rep from * to last 2 sts, p1, k1.
Row 3 Rep row 1.
Row 4 Rep row 2.
Rows 5 and 7 Rep row 2.
Rows 6 and 8 Rep row 1. Rep rows 1-8 for pat st.

BACK
With smaller needles, cast on 114 (126, 138) sts. Work in k1, p1 rib for 2 rows.
Next row (RS) K2, *p2, k2; rep from * to end. Cont in k2, p2 rib as established until piece measures 2"/5cm from beg, inc 1 st at end of last WS row— 115 (127, 139) sts. Change to larger needles. Work in pat st until piece measures 15"/38cm from beg, end with a WS row.

Raglan armhole shaping
Bind off 3 sts at beg of next 2 rows—109 (121, 133) sts.
Dec row (RS) K2, SKP, work in pat to last 4 sts, k2tog, k2. Keeping first and last 3 sts in St st,

work 3 rows even. Rep last 4 rows 7 (6, 5) times more—93 (107, 121) sts. Then, rep dec row every other row 29 (35, 41) times—35 (37, 39) sts. Bind off.

FRONT
Work as for back until there 91 (97, 103) sts and armhole measures approx 3¾(4¼, 4½)"/8 (11, 11.5)cm.

Beg placket opening
Next row (RS) K2, SKP, work pat over 38 (41, 44) sts, join 2nd ball of yarn and bind off center 7 sts, work pat to last 4 sts, k2tog, k2. Cont to work both sides at once, cont armhole shaping as on back, until 28 (29, 30) sts rem each side, end with a WS row.

Neck shaping
Next row (RS) K2, SKP, work to end of first side; on 2nd side, bind off 5 (6, 7) sts, work to last 4 sts, k2tog, k2. Cont to work raglan decs (a total of 6 times more) and bind off on next row for other side of neck, AT SAME TIME, dec 1 st from each neck edge every other row 6 times. After

all shaping, 9 sts rem. Then cont raglan armhole shaping every other row 6 times more—3 sts rem each side. **Next row (RS)** K1, SKP; on 2nd side, k2tog, k1. **Next row** Purl. K2tog on each side and fasten off last st.

SLEEVES

With smaller needles, cast on 50 (54, 58) sts. Work in k1, p1 rib for 2 rows. Then work in k2, p2 rib until piece measures 2"/5cm from beg, inc 1 st at end of last WS row—51 (55, 59) sts. Change to larger needles and cont in pat st, inc 1 st each side (working inc sts into pat) every 6th row 14 (10, 14) times, every 8th row 5 (9, 5) times—89 (93, 97) sts. Work even until piece measures 16$\frac{1}{2}$"/42cm from beg.

Raglan cap shaping

Bind off 3 sts at beg of next 2 rows—83 (87, 91) sts. [Work dec row, then work 3 rows even as for back] 9 (11, 13) times—65 sts. Then, work dec row every other row 27 times—11 sts. Bind off on next RS row.

FINISHING

Block pieces to measurements. Sew raglan caps into raglan armholes.

Placket bands

With smaller needles, pick up and k 9 sts along placket opening.

Row 1 (WS) K1, [p1, k1] 4 times.

Row 2 K2, [p1, k1] 3 times, k1. Rep these 2 rows until band fits to beg of neck shaping. Leave sts on a holder. Sew side of band to right placket opening. Work left placket in same way, only pick up sts behind other band.

Collar

With smaller circular needle, pick up and k 112 (116, 120) sts evenly around neck edge, including sts from holders.

Row 1 (RS of collar) K3, *p2, k2; rep from * to last st, end k1.

Row 2 K1, *p2, k2; rep from *, end p2, k1. Rep last 2 rows 3 times more. Change to larger circular needle and cont in rib until collar measures 4$\frac{1}{2}$"/11.5cm, end with WS of collar.

Next row K2, *p1, k1; rep from * to end. Rep this row once more. Bind off in rib. Sew side and sleeve seams.

MEN'S VERSION

FINISHED MEASUREMENTS

■ Chest 44 (48, 53)"/111.5 (122, 134.5)cm
■ Length 25$\frac{1}{2}$ (26$\frac{1}{2}$, 27$\frac{1}{4}$)"/64.5 (67, 69)cm
■ Upper arm 17 (17 3/4, 18$\frac{1}{2}$)"/43 (45, 47)cm

GAUGE

21 sts and 38 rows to 4"/10cm over pat st using larger needles.
TAKE TIME TO CHECK YOUR GAUGE.

PATTERN STITCH

(multiple of 4 sts plus 3 see chart)

BACK

Work as for Women's version back.

FRONT

Work as for back, including raglan armhole shaping, until 63 (65, 67) sts rem and armhole

measures approx 6$\frac{3}{4}$ (7$\frac{1}{2}$, 8$\frac{1}{2}$)"/17 (19, 21.5)cm

Neck shaping

Next row (RS) K2, SKP, work next 19 sts, join 2nd ball of yarn and bind off center 17 (19, 21) sts, work to last 4 sts, k2tog, k2. Cont with raglan armhole shaping on every other row, cont to shape neck by dec 1 st from neck edge on next 2 rows then every other row 5 times more—9 sts. Then cont raglan armhole shaping only every other row 6 times more—3 sts rem each side.

Next row (RS) K1, SKP; on 2nd side, k2tog, k1.

Next row Purl. K2tog on each side and fasten off last st.

SLEEVES

Work as for Women's sleeves, ONLY, inc 1 st each side every 8th row 19 times—89 (93, 97) sts. Work even until piece measures 19"/48cm from beg.

Raglan cap shaping

Work as for Women's raglan cap shaping.

FINISHING

Block pieces to measurements. Sew raglan caps into raglan armholes.

Neckband

With RS facing and smaller circular needle, pick up and k 120 (124, 128) sts evenly around neck edge. Join and work in k2, p2 rib for 7 rnds. Then, work in k1, p1 rib for 2 rnds more. Bind off in rib. Sew side and sleeve seams.

WOMEN'S VERSION

MEN'S VERSION

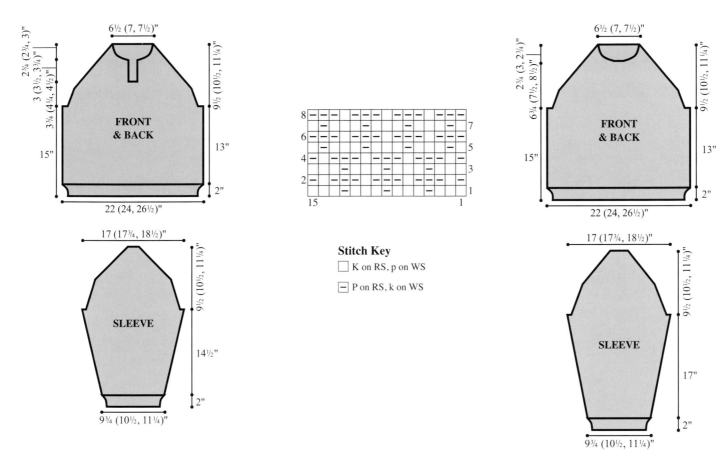

Stitch Key

☐ K on RS, p on WS

— P on RS, k on WS

Country Comforts
for intermediate knitters

Home is certainly where the heart is, especially with delightful matching motif pullovers for mother and daughter. Mom's pullover features cascades of cables with a quaint village scene while the little girl's interpretation highlights just a single house. "Country Comforts" was first featured in the Fall '96 issue of *Family Circle Knitting* magazine.

MATERIALS

Women's version
- *Paterna* by Reynolds/JCA, 1¾oz/50g, each approx 110yd/100m
  11 (11, 12) skeins of #473 taupe (MC), 1 skein each in #10 cream, #717 blue, #715 dk blue, #808 crimson, #142 grey, #815 brick, #847 rust, #912 hunter green, #917 moss green
- *Paternayan Persian* by Reynolds/JCA, each approx 8yd/7.35m, used doubled
  5 skeins of #411 brown

Child's version
- *Paterna* by Reynolds/JCA, 1¾oz/50g, each approx 110yd/100m
  5 (6) skeins of #473 taupe (MC), 1 skein or less each in #10 cream, #142 grey, #717 blue, #715 dk blue, #808 crimson, #815 brick, #847 rust, #912 hunter green, #917 moss green
- *Paternayan Persian* by Reynolds/JCA each 8yd/7.35m, used doubled
  4 skeins of #411 brown

Both versions
- One pair size 9 (5.5mm) needles OR SIZE TO OBTAIN GAUGE
- Cable needle
- Tapestry needle

SIZES

Child's sweater
Sized for children's 4-6 (8-10). Shown in size 4-6.
Women's sweater
Sized for Small (Medium, Large). Shown in size Medium.

CHILD'S SWEATER

FINISHED MEASUREMENTS
- Chest 30 (34)"/76 (86.5)cm
- Length 18 (21)"/45.5 (53.5)cm
- Width at upper arm 11 (12)"/28 (30.5)cm

GAUGE
20 sts and 24 rows to 4"/10cm over St st with size 9 (5.5)needle. TAKE TIME TO CHECK YOUR GAUGE.

STITCH GLOSSARY

6-st RC
Sl 3 sts to cn and hold to back of work, k 3, k 3 from cn

6-st Right Cable
Rows 1 and 5 (RS) K 6 Rows 2 and 4 P 6
Rows 3 (RS)
6-st RC Row 6 Rep row 2. Rep Rows 1-6 for 6-st Right Cable.

Note
When changing color, pick up new color from under previous color on WS to prevent holes.

BACK
With MC , cast on 72 (84) sts.

Rib
Row 1 (RS) K 1, *p 2, row 1 of 6-st Right Cable, p 2, k 2, *rep between *'s to last 11 sts, p 2, row 1 of 6-st Right Cable, p 2, k 1.
Row 2 P 1, *k 2, row 2 of 6-st Right Cable, k 2, p 2*, rep between *'s to last 11 sts, k 2, row 2 of 6-st Right Cable, k 2, p 1.
Rows 3-6 Rep Rows 1 and 2, cont 6-st Right cable pat as established. Beg Village chart Work chart rows 1-13 in St st. Change to MC, cont in St st until piece measures 12 (14)"/30.5 (35.5)cm from beg.

Armhole shaping
Bind off 2 sts at beg of next 2 rows, then dec 1 st each side every other row 3 times – 62 (74) sts. Work until armholes measure 6 (7)"/15 (18)cm.

Shoulder shaping
Bind off 10 (11) sts at beg of next 2 rows, 10 (12) sts at beg of next 2 rows. Bind off rem 22 (28) sts.

FRONT
With MC, cast on 72 (84) sts. Work rib rows as for back dec 1 st end of last row–71 (83) sts. Beg village chart rows 1-13 in St st. Cont in St st working the House chart on center of front.

Work until piece measures same as back to underarm, work with MC only after House motif has been completed.

Armhole shaping

Shape armholes same as back and work until armholes measure 4¹/₂ (5)"/11.5 (12.5)cm, ending with a WS row.

Neck shaping

Next row (RS) Work on 24 (28) sts, join 2nd ball of yarn and bind off center 13 (17) sts, finish row. Working both sides at once, bind off from each neck edge 2 sts 1 (2) times, 1 st 2 (1) times—20 (23) sts each side. Cont until same length as back.

Shoulder shaping

Shape shoulders same as back.

SLEEVES

With MC , cast on 36 sts.

Rows 1-6 Rep rib rows 1-6 of back. Foll village chart 1-13 in St st. Change to MC, AT SAME TIME, inc 1 st each side every 6th row 10 (12) times—56 (60) sts. Work until sleeves measures 13 (14)"/33 (35.5)cm from beg or desired length to underarm, ending with a WS row.

Cap shaping

Bind off 2 sts at beg of next 2 rows, then dec 1 st each side every other row 3 times. Bind off remaining 46 (50) sts.

FINISHING

Sew right shoulder seam. With MC pick up 84 (96) sts evenly around neck edge. Rep rib rows 1-5 of back. Bind off in rib. Sew left shoulder and neckband seam. Sew in sleeves. Sew side and sleeve seams. Embroider French knots on border.

HOUSE CHART

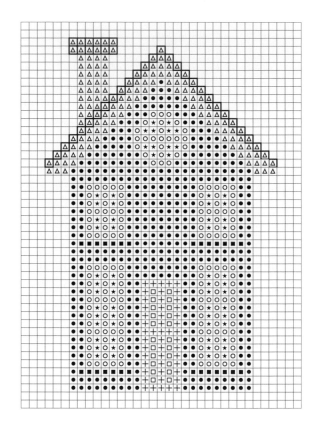

 Brown

★ Grey

+ Hunter green

□ Moss green

△ Brown

• Crimson

△ Rust

WOMEN'S SWEATER

FINISHED MEASUREMENTS
- Bust 43 (48, 53)"/109 (122, 134.5)cm
- Length 28 (28 1/2, 29)"/71 (72.5, 73.5)cm
- Width at upper arm 14 (15, 16)"/35.5 (38, 40.5)cm

GAUGE
20 sts and 24 rows to 1"/2.5cm over St st. TAKE TIME TO CHECK YOUR GAUGE.

Note
Cable sts will have a tighter gauge varying with the row.

STITCH
6-st RC
Sl 3 sts to cn and hold to back of work, k 3, k 3 from cn

8-st RC
Sl 4 sts to cn and hold to back of work, k 4, k 4 from cn

6-st Right Cable
Rows 1 and 5 (RS) K 6. Rows 2, 4 and 6 P 6
Rows 3 and 7 (RS) 6-st RC. Row 8 Rep row 2
Rep Rows 1-8 for 6-st Right Cable.

8-st Right Cable
Rows 1, 3 and 7 (RS) K 8. Rows 2, 4 and 6 P 8.
Row 5 8-st RC. **Row 8** Rep row 2
Rep Rows 1-8 for 8-st Right Cable.

Notes
Only colors in Paternayan Persian are worked with a double strand. All others colors are with a worked single strand.

BACK
With MC, cast on 108 (120, 132) sts.
Rib
Row 1 (RS) K 1, *p 2, row 1 of 6-st Right Cable, p 2, k 2, *rep between *'s to last 11 sts, p 2, row 1 of 6-st Right Cable, p 2, k 1.
Row 2 P 1, *k 2, row 2 of 6-st Right Cable, k 2, p 2*, rep between *'s to last 11 sts, k 2, row 2 of 6-st Right Cable, k 2, p 1.
Rows 3-8 Rep Rows 1 and 2 of rib and cont 6-st Right cable pat as established. Beg Village chart rows 1-13 in St st. Then continue with MC only in reverse St st until piece measures 19"/48.5cm from beg.

Armhole shaping
Bind off 2 sts at beg of next 4 rows, then dec 1 st each side every other row 3 times—94 (106, 118) sts. Work until armholes measure 9 (9½, 10)"/23 (24, 25.5)cm.

Shoulder shaping
Bind off 9 (11, 12) sts at beg of next 6 rows. Bind off remaining 40 (40, 46) sts.

FRONT
With MC, cast on 108 (120, 132) sts.
Beg rib rows
Work rib rows as for back.
Beg village chart
Beg with row 1, foll chart in St st to top of chart—row 60. Rep bottom border reading from row 13-1, ending with a WS row.
Establish Cable Pat
Row 1 P 5 (8, 11), *row 1 of 8-st Right Cable, p 7 (8, 9)*, rep between *'s to last 13 (16, 19) sts, end row 1 of 8-st Right Cable, p 5 (8, 11)
Row 2 K 5 (8, 11), *row 2 of 8-st Right Cable, k 7 (8, 9)*, rep between *'s to last 13 (16, 19) sts, row 2 of 8-st Right Cable, k 5 (8, 11). Work in est pat as established cont 8-st Right Cable until piece measures same as back to underarm.
Armhole shaping
Cont in Cable pat, shape armholes same as back and work until armholes measure 6½ (7, 7½)"/16.5 (18, 19)cm, ending with a WS row.

Neck shaping
Next row (RS) Work 37 (43, 47) sts in est pat, join 2nd ball of yarn and bind off center 20 (20, 24) sts, finish row. Working both sides at once, bind off from each neck edge 3 sts twice, 2 sts once, 1 st 2 (2, 3) times—27 (33, 36) sts each side. Cont until same length as back.

Shoulder shaping
Shape shoulders same as back.

SLEEVES
With MC, cast on 48 sts. Work rib rows as for back. Beg village chart working first 48 sts, foll chart rows 1-13 in St st, ending with a WS row.
Est Cable Pat
Row 1 (RS) P 5 (4, 3), *row 1 of 8-st Right Cable, p 7 (8, 9)*, rep between *'s twice more, row 1 of 8-st Right Cable, p 5 (4, 3).
Row 2 K 5 (4, 3), *row 2 of 8-st Right Cable, k 7 (8, 9)*, rep between *'s twice more, row 2 of 8-st Right Cable, k 5 (4, 3). Cont in pat as established, inc 1 st each side every 6th row 12 (14, 16) times working added sts in reverse St st—72 (76, 80) sts. Cont until sleeves measure 18 (19, 19)"/45.5 (48.5, 48.5)cm from beg or desired length to underarm, ending with a WS row.

Cap shaping
Bind off 2 sts at beg of next 4 rows, then dec 1 st each side every other row 2 (2, 3) times. Bind off remaining 60 (64, 66) sts.

FINISHING
Sew right shoulder seam. With MC pick up 108 (108, 120) sts evenly around neck edge. Rep rib rows 1-5 of back. Bind off in rib. Sew left shoulder and neckband seam. Sew in sleeves. Sew side and sleeve seams. Embroider French knots on border.

CHILD'S VERSION

WOMEN'S VERSION

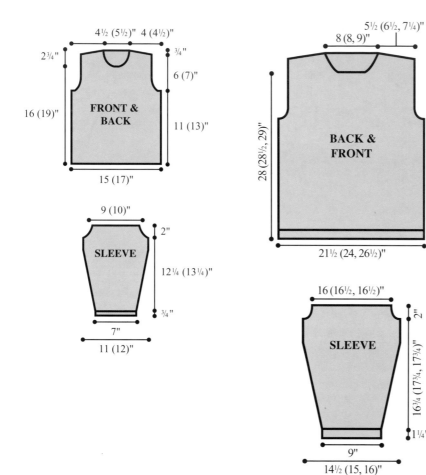

4½ (5½)" 4 (4½)"

2¾"

¾"

6 (7)"

16 (19)"

FRONT &
BACK

11 (13)"

15 (17)"

9 (10)"

2"

SLEEVE

12¼ (13¼)"

¾"

7"

11 (12)"

5½ (6½, 7¼)"

8 (8, 9)"

1"

9 (9½, 10)"

28 (28½, 29)"

BACK &
FRONT

17¾"

1¼"

21½ (24, 26½)"

16 (16½, 16½)"

2"

SLEEVE

16¾ (17¾, 17¾)"

1¼"

9"

14½ (15, 16)"

☐ #473 Taupe (MC)

L #847 Rust

△ #411 Brown

V #847 Rust

▲ #715 Dk. Blue

✕ #717 Blue

⬤ #808 Crimson

▢ #917 Moss Green

◯ #10 Cream

★ #142 Grey

╱ #815 Brick

✛ #912 Hunter Green

VILLAGE CHART

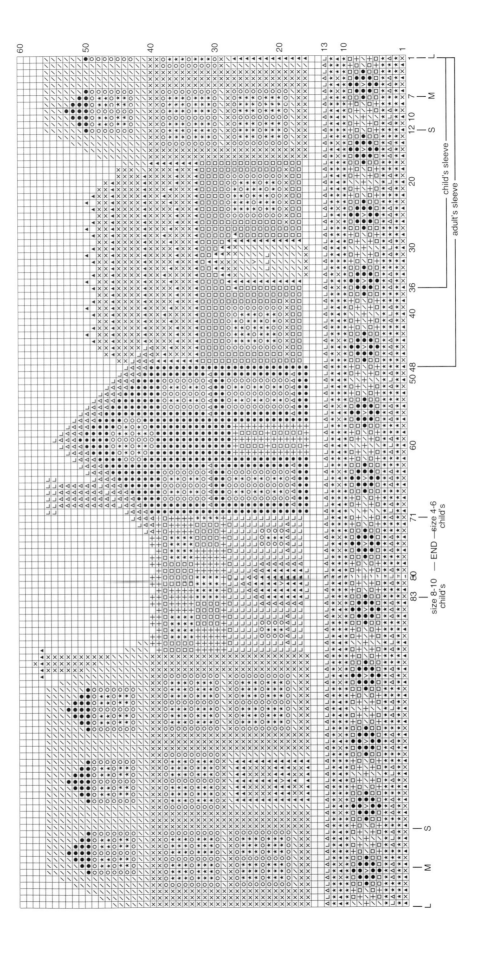

Tree Toppers

for beginner kniters

With rolled necks, cuffs, and hem, these handsome father-and-son fir tree-motif sweaters chase away the chills and brighten up the holidays. Rolled-edge, striped hat for the boy tops it off. Designed by Linda Cyr, "Tree Toppers" first appeared in the Fall '96 issue of *Family Circle Knitting* magazine.

MATERIALS

Child's version

- *Aspen Soft* by Bernat®, 5oz/140g, each approx 275yd/253m (acrylic & wool)
  4 (4, 5, 5) skeins #4901 cream (MC), 1 skein each #4907 pine (CC)

Men's version

  7 (7, 8) skeins #4907 pine (MC), 1 skein each #4901 cream (CC)

Both versions

- One pair size 7 (4.5mm) needles OR SIZE TO OBTAIN GAUGE
- Size 7 (4.5mm) circular needle 16"/40cm long
- Stitch holder and stitch markers
- Tapestry needle

Hat

  1 skein each #4907 pine (MC) and #4901 cream (CC)

- One set (4) double-pointed needles size

SIZES

Child's version

Sized for children's size 4 (6, 8, 10). Shown in size 6.

Men's version

Sized for adult's Medium (Large, X-Large). Shown in size Large.

Rolled edge hat

Sized for child (adult). Shown in child size.

CHILD'S VERSION

FINISHED MEASUREMENTS

- Chest 32 (34, 36, 38)"/81.5 (86.5, 91.5, 96.5)cm
- Length 17½ (18½, 20, 22)"/44.5 (47, 51, 56)cm
- Width at upperarm 14¾ (15½, 16, 17)"/37.5 (39.5, 40.5, 43)cm

GAUGE

20 sts and 26 rows to 4"/10cm over St st using size 7 (4½mm) needles.
TAKE TIME TO CHECK GAUGE.

Notes

Finished measurements allow for approx 1"/2.5cm rolled edges.

BACK

With MC and size 7 (4.5mm) needles, cast on 81 (85, 91, 95) sts. Work in St st until piece measures 18½ (19½, 21, 23"/47 (49.5, 53.5, 58.5)cm from beg, ending with a WS row. Bind off all sts.

FRONT

Work as for back until piece measures 6½ (7, 7½, 8)/16.5 (17.5, 19, 20.5)cm from beg, ending with a WS row. Beg chart:

Next row (RS) K29 (31, 34, 36) sts. Cont in St st working until chart has been completed. Cont with MC only until piece measures 16¼ (17¼, 18¾, 20¾)"/41.5 (44, 47.5, 52.5)cm from beg, ending with a WS row.

Neck shaping

Next row (RS) K 34 (35, 37, 38), sl center 13 (15, 17, 19) sts to holder, join 2nd ball of yarn and work rem 34 (35, 37, 38) sts. Working both sides at once, bind off from each neck edge 3 sts once, 2 sts twice, 1 st twice. When same length as back, bind off rem 25 (26, 28, 29) sts each side.

SLEEVES

With MC and size 7 (4.5mm) needles, cast on 38 (38, 40, 40) sts. Work even in St st for 1"/2.5cm, ending with a WS row. Cont in St st, inc 1 st each side every 4th row 14 (17, 13, 16) times, then every 6th row 4 (3, 7, 6) times—74 (78, 80, 84) sts. Work even until piece measures 13½ (14½, 16, 17)"/34.5 (37, 38, 43)cm from beg, ending with a WS row. Bind off all sts.

FINISHING

Sew shoulder seams. Collar With RS facing, MC and circular needle, pick up and k 76 (80, 84, 90) sts around neck edge. Join, work in rnds:

Rnd 1 P. Mark center back. Cont in k, dec 1 st before and after marker every other rnd 3 times—70 (74, 78, 84) sts. Work even in k until collar measures 2"/5cm or desired length. Bind

off all sts. Place markers 7½ (7¾, 8, 8½)"/19 (19.5, 20.5, 21.5)cm from shoulder seams. Sew top of sleeves bet markers. Sew side and sleeve seams.

MEN'S VERSION

FINISHED MEASUREMENTS
- Chest 46 (48, 50)"/116.5 (122, 127)cm
- Length 26 (26½, 27)"/66 (67.5, 68.5)
- Width at upper arm 16(17,18)"/40.5(43, 45.5)cm

GAUGE
20 sts and 26 rows to 4"/10cm over St st using size 7 (4.5mm) needles
TAKE TIME TO CHECK GAUGE

Notes
Finished measurements allow for approx 1"/2.5cm rolled edges.

BACK
With MC and size 7(4.5mm) needles, cast on 115(121,125)sts. Work in St st until piece measures 17"/43cm from beg, ending with a WS row.

Armhole shaping
Bind off 4 sts at beg of next 2 rows. Dec 1 st each side every RS row 5 times—97 (103, 107) sts. Work even until piece measures 26 (26¾, 27)"/66 (67.5, 68.5)cm from beg.

Shoulder shaping
Bind off 7 (8, 8) sts at beg of next 4 rows, 7 (7, 8) sts at beg of next 4 rows. Bind off rem 41 (43, 43) sts.

FRONT
Work as for back until piece measures 12¾(13¾, 13¾)"/32.5 (35, 35) cm from beg, ending with a WS row.

Beg chart
Next row (RS) K 43 (46, 48), beg with row 1 work next 29 sts foll chart (joining ball of CC to 2nd ball of MC), k 43 (46, 48). Cont in St st working until chart has been completed. AT THE SAME TIME, when piece measures 17"/43cm from beg, shape armholes as for

back. Cont with MC only until piece measures 25 (25½, 26)"/63.5 (65, 66)cm from beg, ending with a WS row.

Neck shaping
Next row (RS) K 40 (42, 44), sl center 17 (19, 19) sts to holder, join 2nd ball of yarn and work rem 40 (42, 44) sts. Working both sides at once, bind off from each neck edge 3 sts twice, 2 sts twice, 1 st twice—28 (30, 32) sts each side. When same length as for back, shape shoulders as on back.

SLEEVES
With MC and size 7 (4.5mm) needles, cast on 42 (44, 46) sts. Work even in St st for 1"/2.5cm, ending with a WS row. Cont in St st, inc 1 st each side every 6th row 12 (16, 18) times, then every 8th row 7 (5, 4) times—80 (86, 90) sts. Work even until piece measures 21½ (22, 22½)"/54.5 (56, 57)cm from beg, ending with a WS row.

Cap shaping
Bind off 4 sts at beg of next 2 rows. Dec 1 st each side every row 8 times, every other row 3 times, then every row 6 times. Bind off 2 sts at beg of next 12 rows. Bind off rem 14 (20, 24) sts.

FINISHING
Sew shoulder seams. Collar With RS facing, using MC and circular needle, pick up and k 108 (112, 112) sts around neck edge. Join and work in rnds as foll:
Rnd 1: P. Mark center back. Cont around in k, dec 1 st before and after marker every other rnd 3 times—102 (106, 106) sts. Work even in k until collar measures 3"/7cm or desired length. Bind off all sts. Sew in sleeves. Sew side and sleeve seams.

HAT

FINISHED MEASUREMENTS
- Circumference: 19½ (21)"/48.5(52.5)cm

GAUGE
20 sts and 26 rows to 4"/10cm over St st using size 7 (4.5mm) needles

Note
Color not being used is twisted in every few rows to avoid a long loop.

HAT
With size 7 (4.5mm) dpns and MC, cast on 98 (105) sts. Divide sts on 3 dpns. Join and place marker for beg of rnd. Work in alternate stripes of 12 rnds MC, 12 rnds CC until piece measures 5½ (6½)"/14 (16.5)cm from beg.

Crown shaping
Dec rnd: Dec 7 sts evenly spaced around —91 (98) sts. Work dec rnd every 4 rnds until 14 sts rem. Cut yarn leaving a tail, draw end through rem sts.

FINISHING
With MC, make a pompom 2½"/6.5cm. Attach to top of hat.

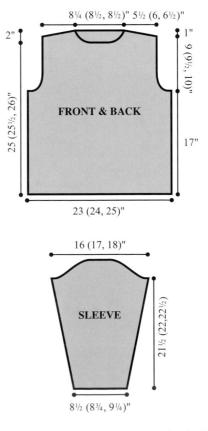

MEN'S SWEATER

8¼ (8½, 8½)" 5½ (6, 6½)"

2" 1"

9 (9½, 10)"

FRONT & BACK

25 (25½, 26)"

17"

23 (24, 25)"

16 (17, 18)"

SLEEVE

21½ (22,22½)"

8½ (8¾, 9¼)"

CHILD'S SWEATER

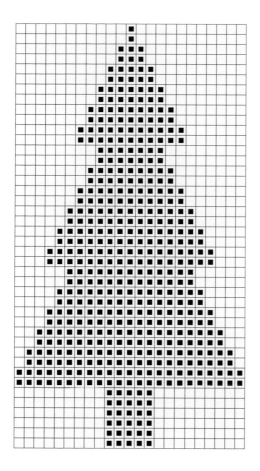

MEN'S SWEATER

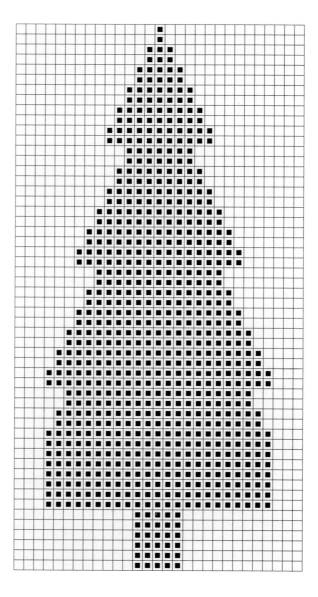

CHILD'S SWEATER

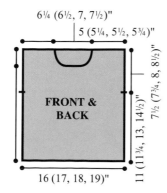

6¼ (6½, 7, 7½)"

5 (5¼, 5½, 5¾)"

7½ (7¾, 8, 8½)"

FRONT &
BACK

11 (11¾, 13, 14½)"

16 (17, 18, 19)"

14¼ (15½, 16, 17)"

SLEEVE

13½ (14½, 16, 17)"

7½ (7½, 8, 8)"

Winter Warmers

for beginner knitters

Barbara Khouri works simple shaping, basic stitches, and muted colors into delicate mother-and-daughter cardigans. Whimsical snowflake and tree motifs are sure to banish winter doldrums. "Winter Warmers" first appeared in the Winter '98/'99 issue of *Family Circle Easy Knitting* magazine.

MATERIALS

Child's version
- *Eternity* by Reynolds/JCA, 1³⁄₄oz/50g balls, each approx 88yd/81m (wool/microfiber)
  4 (4, 5) balls in #835 lt blue (B) and 2 (2, 3) balls in #845 lt green (A)
- *Chateau* by Reynolds/JCA, 1³⁄₄oz/50g balls, each approx 136yd/122m (wool/nylon/ angora)
  1 ball in #1 white (C)

Women's version
- *Eternity* by Reynolds/JCA
  10 (11, 12, 14) balls in #835 lt blue (B) and 3 (3, 4, 4) balls in #845 lt green (A)
- Chateau by Reynolds/JCA
  2 balls in #1 white (C)

Both versions
- Five ³⁄₄"/20mm buttons for child's sweater
- Six ³⁄₄"/20mm buttons for women's sweater
- One pair each sizes 6 and 8 (4 and 5mm) needles OR SIZE TO OBTAIN GAUGE
- Stitch holders

SIZES

Child's version
Sized for Girl's sizes 2(4, 6). Shown in size 4.
Women's version
Sized for Small (Medium, Large, X-Large). Shown in size Medium.

CHILD'S VERSION

FINISHED MEASUREMENTS

- Chest (buttoned) 22¹⁄₂ (27, 30¹⁄₂)"/57 (68.5, 77.5)cm
- Length 11¹⁄₂ (12¹⁄₂, 13¹⁄₂)"/29 (32, 34.5)cm
- Upper arm 9¹⁄₂ (10¹⁄₂, 11¹⁄₂)"/24 (27, 29)cm

GAUGE

19 sts and 20 rows to 4"/10cm over St st and chart pat using larger needles.
TAKE TIME TO CHECK YOUR GAUGE.

Note

When changing colors, twist yarns tog on WS to prevent holes. Carry yarn loosely across WS to prevent puckering.

BACK

With smaller needles and A, cast on 53 (63, 71) sts.
Row 1 (RS) K1, *p1, k1; rep from * to end. Work in k1, p1 rib as established (k the knit sts and p the purl sts) until piece measures 1¹⁄₂"/3.5cm from beg, end with a RS row. Change to larger needles and p 1 row on WS.

Beg chart

Row 1 (RS) Foll row 1 of chart, beg as indicated, work 14-st rep 3 (3, 5) times, end as indicated. Cont to foll chart through row 33, then rep rows 18-33 to end of piece, and when piece measures 10¹⁄₂ (11¹⁄₂, 12¹⁄₂)"/26.5 (29, 32)cm from beg, work neck shaping.

Neck shaping

Next row (RS) Work 20 (24, 28) sts, join a 2nd ball of yarn and bind off center 13 (15, 15) sts, work to end. Working both sides at once with separate balls of yarn, bind off 2 sts from each neck edge twice. When piece measures 11¹⁄₂ (12¹⁄₂, 13¹⁄₂)"/29 (32, 34.5)cm from beg, bind off rem 16 (20, 24) sts each side for shoulders.

LEFT FRONT

With smaller needles and A, cast on 32 (38, 42) sts.
Row 1 (RS) *K1, p1; rep from * to last 2 sts, k2.
Row 2 P2, *k1, p1; rep from * to end. Work in k1, p1 rib as established for 1¹⁄₂"/3.5cm, end with a RS row.
Next row (WS) Work first 7 sts in rib and sl to a holder for front band, change to larger needles and p to end, inc 1 (0, 0) st—26 (31, 35) sts.

Beg chart

Row 1 (RS) Foll row 1 of chart, beg as indicated, work 14-st rep once, end as indicated. Cont to foll chart through row 33, then rep rows 18-33 to end of piece and when piece measures 10 (11, 12)"/25.5 (28, 30.5)cm from beg, work neck shaping.

Neck shaping

Next row (WS) Bind off 4 sts, work to end. Cont to bind off 4 sts from neck edge once, 2 (3, 3) sts once. When same length as back, bind off rem 16 (20, 24) sts for shoulder.

RIGHT FRONT

Cast on and work to correspond to left front, reversing placement of front band, until piece measures ¾"/2cm from beg.
Buttonhole row (RS) Work 4 sts, yo, k2tog, work to end. Cont to work as for left front reversing shaping and pat placement.

SLEEVES

With smaller needles and A, cast on 27 (29, 31) sts. Work in rib as for back for 1"/2.5cm. Change to larger needles and p 1 row on WS. Centering st as indicated on chart, work in chart pat as for back, AT SAME TIME, inc 1 st each side every 4th row 9 (10, 12) times—45 (49, 55) sts. Work even until piece measures 13"/33cm from beg. Bind off.

FINISHING

Block pieces to measurements. Sew shoulder seams. With smaller needles and A, work across 7 sts from left front holder, inc 1 st at inside edge (for seaming). Work in rib (changing to B to match front), until band fits to neck shaping, stretching slightly. Bind off. Sew to front edge. Place markers for 4 buttons, the top one at ½"/1.25cm from top, the lower one at 2"/5cm from first buttonhole in lower band and the others evenly spaced between. Work right front band to correspond, working 4 more yo, k2tog buttonholes to correspond to first one in lower rib. Sew to right front.

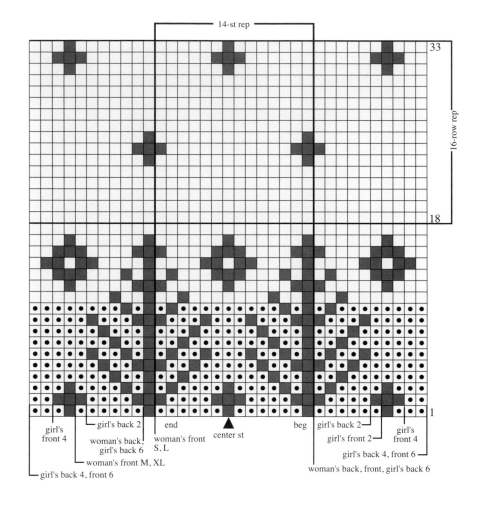

Color Key

- ● Lt. green (A)
- □ Lt. blue (B)
- ■ White (C)

Collar

With RS facing, smaller needles and B, pick up and k 71 (75, 75) sts evenly around neck edge. **Row 1 (WS)** P2, *k1, p1, rep from *, end p2. Work in rib as established for $2\frac{1}{2}$"/6.5cm. Bind off in rib. Place markers at $4\frac{3}{4}$($5\frac{1}{4}$, $5\frac{3}{4}$)"/12 (13.5, 14.5)cm down from shoulders. Sew sleeves to armholes between markers. Sew side and sleeve seams. Sew on buttons.

WOMEN'S VERSION

FINISHED MEASUREMENTS

■ Bust (buttoned) $36\frac{1}{2}$ ($42\frac{1}{2}$, $47\frac{1}{2}$, $53\frac{1}{2}$)"/92.5 (108, 120.5, 136)cm
■ Length $20\frac{1}{2}$ (21, $21\frac{1}{2}$, 22)"/52 (53.5, 54.5, 56)cm
■ Upper arm $16\frac{1}{4}$ (18, 19, $20\frac{1}{2}$)"/41.5 (45.5, 48, 52)cm

GAUGE

19 sts and 20 rows to 4"/10cm over St st and chart pat using larger needles.
TAKE TIME TO CHECK YOUR GAUGE.

Note

When changing colors, twist yarns tog on WS to prevent holes. Carry yarn loosely across WS to prevent puckering.

BACK

With smaller needles and A, cast on 85 (99, 113, 127) sts.
Row 1 (RS) K1, *p1, k1; rep from * to end. Work in k1, p1 rib as established (k the knit and p the purl sts) until piece measures $1\frac{1}{2}$"/3.5cm from beg, end with a RS row. Change to larger needles and p 1 row on WS.

Beg chart

Row 1 (RS) Foll row 1 of chart, beg as indicated, work 14-st rep 6 (7, 8, 9) times, end as indicated. Cont to foll chart through row 33, then rep rows 18-33 to end of piece, and work until piece measures 11"/28cm from beg.

Armhole shaping

Bind off 3 (4, 5, 6) sts at beg of next 2 rows, 3 sts at beg of next 2 (2, 2, 4) rows, 2 sts at beg of next 2 (2, 4, 4) rows.
Next (dec) row (RS) K1, k2tog, work to last 3 sts, ssk, k1. Rep dec row every other row 0 (4, 5, 4) times more—67 (71, 77, 85) sts. Work even until armhole measures $8\frac{1}{2}$ (9, $9\frac{1}{2}$, 10)"/21.5 (23, 24, 25.5)cm.

Neck and shoulder shaping

Bind off 6 (7, 8, 9) sts at beg of next 4 rows, 7 (7, 7, 8) sts at beg of next 2 rows, AT SAME TIME, bind off center 21 (21, 23, 25) sts and working both sides at once with separate balls of yarn, bind off 2 sts from each neck edge twice.

LEFT FRONT

With smaller needles and A, cast on 48 (56, 62, 70) sts.
Row 1 (RS) *K1, p1; rep from * to last 2 sts, k2.
Row 2 P2, *k1, p1; rep from * to end. Work in k1, p1 rib as established for $1\frac{1}{2}$"/3.5cm, end with a RS row.
Next row (WS) Work first 7 sts in rib and sl to a holder for front band, change to larger needles and p to end, inc 1 (0, 1, 0) st—42 (49, 56, 63) sts.

Beg chart

Row 1 (RS) Foll row 1 of chart, beg as indicated, work 14-st rep 3 (3, 4, 4) times, end as indicated. Cont to foll chart through row 33, then rep rows 18-33 to end of piece and work until piece measures 11"/28cm from beg.

Armhole shaping

Work as for back armhole shaping at beg of RS rows—33 (35, 38, 42) sts. Work even until armhole measures $6\frac{1}{2}$ (7, $7\frac{1}{2}$, 8)"/16.5 (18, 19, 20.5)cm, end with a RS row.

Neck shaping

Next row (RS) Bind off 4 (4, 4, 5) sts, work to end. Cont to bind off from neck edge 3 sts twice, 2 sts once.
Next row (RS) K to last 4 sts, ssk, k2. Rep this row every other row 1 (1, 2, 2) times more, AT SAME TIME, when same length as back, shape shoulders as for back.

RIGHT FRONT

Work to correspond to left front, reversing placement of front band, until piece measures $\frac{3}{4}$"/2cm from beg.
Buttonhole row (RS) Work 4 sts, yo, k2tog, work to end. Cont to work as for left front reversing shaping and pat placement.

SLEEVES

With smaller needle and A, cast on 43 (43, 45, 45) sts. Work in rib as for back for $1\frac{1}{2}$"/3.5cm. Change to larger needles and p 1 row on WS. Centering st as indicated, work in chart pat as on back, AT SAME TIME, inc 1 st each side every 4th row 9 (21, 19, 16) times, every 6th (0, 2nd, 2nd) row 8 (0, 4, 10) times—77 (85, 91, 97) sts. Work even until piece measures $19\frac{1}{4}$"/49cm from beg.

Cap shaping

Bind off 3 (4, 5, 6) sts at beg of next 2 rows, 3 sts at beg of next 2 rows, 2 sts at beg of next 4 rows. Bind off rem 57 (63, 67, 71) sts.

FINISHING

Block pieces to measurements. Sew shoulder seams. With smaller needles and A, work across 7 sts from left front holder, inc 1 st at inside edge (for seaming). Work in rib (changing to B to match front) until band fits to neck shaping, stretching slightly. Bind off. Sew to front edge. Place markers for 5 buttons evenly spaced, the top one at ¹⁄₂"/1.25cm from top, the lower one at beg of color change to B and the others evenly spaced between. Work right front band to correspond, working 5 more yo, k2tog buttonholes to correspond to first one in lower rib. Sew to right front.

Collar

With RS facing, smaller needles and B, pick up and k 89 (89, 93, 97) sts evenly around neck edge.

Row 1 (WS) P2, *k1, p1; rep from *, end p2. Work in rib as established for 3¹⁄₂"/9cm. Bind off in rib. Sew sleeves into armholes. Sew side and sleeve seams. Sew on buttons.

CHILD'S VERSION

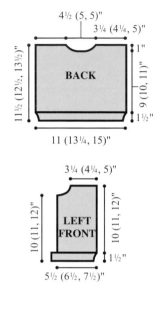

BACK

4½ (5, 5)"
3¼ (4¼, 5)"
11½ (12½, 13½)"
1"
9 (10, 11)"
1½"
11 (13¼, 15)"

LEFT FRONT

3¼ (4¼, 5)"
10 (11, 12)"
10 (11, 12)"
1½"
5½ (6½, 7½)"

SLEEVE

9½ (10½, 11½)"
12"
1"
5½ (6, 6½)"

WOMEN'S VERSION

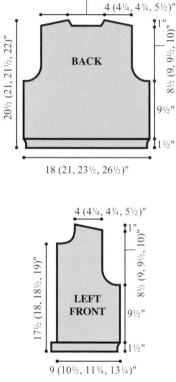

BACK

6 (6, 6½, 7)"
4 (4¼, 4¾, 5½)"
20½ (21, 21½, 22)"
1"
8½ (9, 9½, 10)"
9½"
1½"
18 (21, 23½, 26½)"

LEFT FRONT

4 (4¼, 4¾, 5½)"
1"
8½ (9, 9½, 10)"
17½ (18, 18½, 19)"
9½"
1½"
9 (10½, 11¾, 13¼)"

SLEEVE

16¼ (18, 19, 20½)"
1½"
17¾"
1½"
9 (9, 9½, 9½)"

Vested Interests

for intermediate knitters

Simple tweed linen-stitch vests are exactly right for the holidays. Grandpa's button-down V-neck perfectly complements his grandson's zip-front, navy-edged version. Both designed by Mary Marik, "Vested Interests" first appeared in the Winter '99/'00 issue of *Family Circle Easy Knitting* magazine.

MATERIALS

Child's version

■ *8-Ply* by Wool Pak Yarns NZ/Baabajoes Wool Company, 8oz/250g skeins, each approx 525yd/472m (wool)

1 skein each in blue (MC) and natural (CC)

■ One 9"/23cm separating zipper

Men's version

■ *8-Ply* by Wool Pak Yarns NZ/Baabajoes Wool Company, 8oz/250g skeins, each approx 525yd/472m (wool)

2 skeins in green (MC) and 1 skein in natural (CC)

■ Seven ¾"/20mm buttons

Both versions

■ One pair each sizes 7 and 10 (4.5 and 6mm) needles OR SIZE TO OBTAIN GAUGE

■ Size 7 (4.5mm) circular needle, 16"/40cm long

■ Stitch holders and markers

SIZES

Child's version

Sized for Child's 2 (4, 6). Shown in Child's size 4.

Men's version

Sized for Men's Small (Medium, Large). Shown in Men's size Medium.

CHILD'S VERSION

FINISHED MEASUREMENTS

■ Chest 23 (25, 27)"/58.5 (63.5, 68.5)cm

■ Length 13 (14½, 16)"/33 (37, 40.5)cm

GAUGE

22 sts and 40 rows to 4"/10cm over tweed pat st using larger needles.

TAKE TIME TO CHECK YOUR GAUGE.

TWEED PATTERN STITCH

(even number of sts)

Row 1 (RS) With MC, *wyif sl 1 st purlwise, wyib k1; rep from * to end.

Row 2 With MC, *wyib sl 1 st purlwise, wyif p1; rep from * to end.

Row 3 With CC, rep row 1.

Row 4 With CC, rep row 2.

Rep rows 1- 4 for tweed pat st.

Note

All decs are worked on MC rows 1 and 2.

Dec row 1 K2tog, k1, work pat st to last 2 sts, k2tog.

Dec row 2 K2tog at beg and end of row.

These 2 dec rows form the 2-st dec at each end as described in instructions.

BACK

With smaller needles and MC, cast on 60 (64, 70) sts. Work in St st for 4 rows, inc 6 sts evenly spaced on last WS row—66 (70, 76) sts. P next row on RS for turning ridge. Cont in St st for 5 more rows. Change to larger needles and beg and end with a k1 selvage st, cont in tweed pat st until piece measures 7½ (8½, 9)"/19 (21.5, 23)cm from beg, end with pat row 2.

Armhole shaping

Bind off 4 sts at beg of next 2 rows. *With MC, work dec rows 1 and 2 over next 2 rows. With CC, work 2 rows even*. Rep between *'s 3 (3, 4)

times more—42 (46, 48) sts. Work even until armhole measures 5 (5½, 6½)"/12.5 (14, 16.5)cm.

Neck and shoulder shaping

Next row (RS) Work 13 (15, 15) sts, join 2nd ball of yarn and bind off center 16 (16, 18) sts, work to end. Working both sides at once, bind off 2 sts from each neck edge every other row twice. When armhole measures 5½ (6, 7)"/14 (15, 18)cm, sl rem 9 (11, 11) sts to holders each side for shoulders.

LEFT FRONT

With smaller needles and MC, cast on 27 (29, 33) sts. Work in St st for 4 rows, inc 3 sts evenly spaced on last WS row—30 (32, 36) sts. P next row on RS for turning ridge. Cont in St st for 5 more rows. Change to larger needles and beg and end with a k1 selvage st, cont in tweed pat st until piece measures 7½ (8½, 9)"/19 (21.5, 23)cm from beg.

Note

For large size only, beg neck shaping on next row. For small and medium sizes, beg neck

shaping when piece measures 9"/23cm from beg.

Armhole and neck shaping

Work armhole shaping as for beg of RS rows on back and at 9"/23cm, shape neck by [dec 2 sts on MC rows 1 and 2, work 2 rows even] 4 (4, 5) times, work 1 more dec at neck edge—9 (11, 11) sts rem. When same length as back to shoulder, sl rem sts to a holder for shoulders.

RIGHT FRONT

Work to correspond to left front, reversing shaping.

FINISHING

Block pieces to measurements. Weave shoulder seams tog.

Armhole bands

With RS facing, smaller needles and MC, pick up and k 60 (68, 78) sts evenly around each armhole edge. P 1 row, k 1 row, p 1 row, k 1 row. K next row on WS for turning row. K next row dec 6 (6, 8) sts evenly spaced—54 (62, 70) sts. P 1 row, k 1 row, p 1 row. Bind off.

Front bands

With circular needle and MC, pick up and k 162 (180, 204) sts evenly around fronts and back neck. Work in band pat as for armhole band. Fold bands in half to WS and sew in place. Sew in zipper at center front. Sew side seams.

MEN'S VERSION

FINISHED MEASUREMENTS

■ Chest 42 (44, 46)"/106.5 (111.5, 117)cm
■ Length 24¹/₂ (25, 26)"/62 (63.5, 66)cm

GAUGE

22 sts and 40 rows to 4"/10cm over tweed pat st using larger needles.
TAKE TIME TO CHECK YOUR GAUGE.

TWEED PATTERN STITCH

(even number of sts)
Row 1 (RS) With MC, *wyif sl 1 st purlwise, wyib k1; rep from * to end.
Row 2 With MC, *wyib sl 1 st purlwise, wyif p1; rep from * to end.
Row 3 With CC, rep row 1.
Row 4 With CC, rep row 2.
Rep rows 1- 4 for tweed pat st.
Note
All decs are worked on MC rows 1 and 2.
Dec row 1 K2tog, k1, work pat st to last 2 sts, k2tog.
Dec row 2 K2tog at beg and end of row.
These 2 dec rows form the 2-st dec at each end as described in instructions.

BACK

With smaller needles and MC, cast on 104 (108, 114) sts. Work in St st for 4 rows, inc 14 sts evenly spaced on last WS row—118 (122, 128) sts. P next row on RS for turning ridge. Cont in St st for 5 more rows. Change to larger needles and beg and end with a k1 selvage st, cont in tweed pat until piece measures 15 (15¹/₂, 16)"/38 (39.5, 40.5)cm from beg, end with pat row 2.

Armhole shaping

Bind off 6 sts at beg of next 2 rows. *With MC, work dec rows 1 and 2 over next 2 rows. With CC, work 2 rows even*. Rep between *'s 5 (5, 6) times more—82 (86, 88) sts. Work even until armhole measures 9 (9, 9¹/₂)"/23 (23, 24)cm.

Neck and shoulder shaping

Next row (RS) Work 23 (25, 26) sts, join 2nd ball of yarn and bind off center 36 sts, work to end. Working both sides at once, bind off 2 sts from each neck edge every other row twice. When armhole measures 9¹/₂ (9¹/₂, 10)"/24 (24, 25.5)cm, sl rem 19 (21, 22) sts to holders each side for shoulders.

LEFT FRONT

With smaller needles and MC, cast on 52 (54, 58) sts. Work in St st for 4 rows, inc 6 sts evenly spaced on last WS row—58 (60, 64) sts. P next row on RS for turning ridge. Cont in St st for 5 more rows. Change to larger needles and beg and end with a k1 selvage st, cont in tweed pat st until piece measures 15 (15¹/₂, 16)"/38 (39.5, 40.5)cm from beg.

Armhole and neck shaping

Work armhole shaping as for beg of RS rows on back, AT SAME TIME, shape neck at end of RS rows by [dec 2 sts on MC rows 1 and 2, work 2 rows even] 10 (10, 11) times. Then work 1 (1, 0) more dec at neck edge—19 (21, 22) sts rem. When same length as back to shoulder, sl rem sts to a holder for shoulder.

RIGHT FRONT

Work to correspond to left front, reversing shaping.

FINISHING

Block pieces to measurements. Weave shoulder seams tog. Sew side seams.

Armhole bands

With RS facing, circular needle and MC, pick up and k sts around armhole as foll: pick up and k 6 sts from back armhole bound-off sts plus 2 more sts, pm, 14 (14, 16) sts along shaped edge of armhole, pm, 30 (30, 35) sts to shoulder, 30 (30, 35) sts to front armhole shaping, pm 14 (14, 16) sts along shaped edge of armhole, pm 2 more sts from shaped edge then 6 sts from front armhole bound-off sts—104 (104, 118) sts. Join to work in rnds.

Dec rnd 1 *K to 2 sts before marker, slip 2 sts to RH needle knitwise, remove marker, k1, pass 2 slipped sts over the k st (for a double dec), replace marker; rep from * 3 times more, k to end. Cont in rnds of St st, rep dec rnd every other rnd 3 times more. Work 1 rnd even. P next rnd for turning ridge, k1 rnd.

Inc rnd 1 *K to marker, M1, sl marker, k1, M1; rep from *, once more, dec 4 sts evenly over the straight armhole sts, then rep from * twice more and k to end. Rep inc rnd every other rnd (but do not work 4 dec sts along the straight edge) 3 times more. Bind off.

Right front band

With RS facing, circular needle and MC, pick up and k 146 (150, 156) sts along right front to center back neck. Work band as for armbands (without dec and inc rows) only dec 9 sts evenly across the neck sts on the first row after the turning row, and dec 6 sts evenly along the center front sts on the 4th row after the turning row. Bind off. Place markers for 7 buttons evenly, the first one at 1"/2.5cm from lower edge, the last one at the neck shaping, the others spaced evenly between.

Right front band

Work as for left front band, working 7 buttonholes opposite markers on row 4 by binding off 3 sts for each buttonhole and casting on 3 sts on the foll row and working a 2nd buttonhole in the center of the hem rows.

MEN'S VERSION

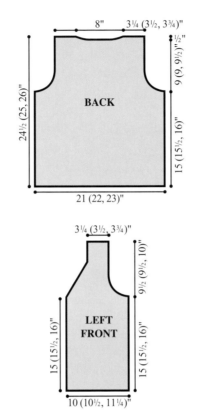

CHILD'S VERSION

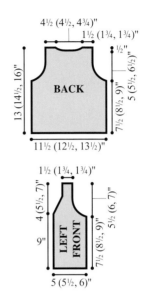

My Mommy and Me

for beginner knitters

Team up for great looks with Melissa Leapman's coordinating sweaters in bands of soft pastel stripes. Mom's relaxed fit cardigan has set-in pockets while little girl's top is a sporty tee. "My Mommy and Me" first appeared in the Spring/Summer '98 issue of *Family Circle Easy Knitting* magazine.

MATERIALS

Child's version

- *Grace* by Patons®, 1¾ oz/50g skeins, each approx 136 yd/125m (cotton)
  2 skeins each in #60321 lilac (A), #60733 aqua (B), #60322 purple (C), #60230 mint (D) and #60130 lt. blue (E)
- One pair size 4 and 6 (3.5 and 4mm) needles OR SIZE TO OBTAIN GAUGE

Women's version

  6 (6, 8) skeins in #17 lilac (A)
  2 (3, 3) skeins each in #71 aqua (B), #108 purple (C), #7 mint (D) and #56 lt. blue (E)
- One pair size 6 (4mm) needles OR SIZE TO OBTAIN GAUGE
- Stitch markers and holders
- Seven ¾"/20mm buttons

CHILD'S VERSION

SIZES

Sized for Child's 2 (4, 6). Shown in size 6.

FINISHED MEASUREMENTS

- Chest 22 (24, 26)"/56 (61, 66)cm
- Length 11 1/2 (12, 13)"/29 (30.5, 33)cm
- Upper arm 10 (10 1/2, 11)"/25.5 (26.5, 28)cm

GAUGE

23 sts and 29 rows to 4"/10cm over St st, using size 6 (4mm) needles.
TAKE TIME TO CHECK YOUR GAUGE.

STITCHES USED

Stripe Pattern

Work in St st (k on RS, p on WS) in foll color sequence: *2 rows B, 3 rows C, 2 rows B, 6 rows A, 1 row D, 3 rows E, 1 row D, 3 rows E, 1 row D, 6 rows A; rep from * (28 rows) for Stripe pat.

BACK

With smaller needles and A, cast on 63 (69, 75) sts. Work in k1, p1 rib for 1"/2.5cm, end with a RS row. Change to larger needles. With A, p 1 row on WS. Work 28 rows of Stripe pat, then work first 8 (8, 12) rows once more. Piece measures approx 6 (6, 6½)"/15 (15, 16.5)cm from beg.

Armhole shaping

Cont pat, bind off 3 (4, 5) sts at beg of next 2 rows. Dec 1 st each side on next row, then every other row twice more—51 (55, 59) sts. Work even until armhole measures 4½ (5, 5½)"/11.5 (12.5, 14)cm, end with a WS row.

Shoulder shaping

Bind off 3 sts at beg of next 8 rows. Bind off rem 27 (31, 35) sts.

FRONT

Work as for back until armhole measures 3½ (4, 4½)"/9 (10, 11.5)cm, end with a WS row.

Neck shaping

Next row (RS) Work 19 (21, 22) sts, join 2nd skein and bind off center 13 (13, 15) sts, work to end. Working both sides at once, bind off from each neck edge 3 sts once, 2 sts 1 (2, 2) times, then dec 1 st at each neck edge every other row 2 (2, 3) times. AT SAME TIME, when same length as back to shoulders, shape shoulders each side for back.

SLEEVES

With smaller needles and A, cast on 47 (49, 51) sts. Work in k1, p1 rib for 1"/2.5cm, end with a WS row. Change to larger needles. Beg with a k row, work in St st as foll: Work 3 rows with A, then work first 8 (8, 12) rows of Stripe pat, AT SAME TIME, inc 1 st each side on first row, then every row 0 (2, 0) times, every other row 4 (3, 5) times—57 (61, 63) sts. Piece measures approx 2½ (2½, 3)"/6.5 (6.5, 7.5)cm from beg.

Cap shaping

Cont in stripe pat, bind off 3 (4, 5) sts at beg of next 2 rows. Dec 1 st each side on next row, then every other row 10 times more. Work 1 row even. Bind off 3 sts at beg of next 6 rows. Bind off rem 11 (13, 13) sts.

FINISHING

Block pieces. Sew right shoulder seam.

Neckband

With RS facing, smaller needles and A, pick up and k 59 (67, 75) sts evenly around neck edge. Work in k1, p1 rib for ³/₄"/2cm. Bind off all sts in rib pat. Sew left shoulder seam, including neckband. Set in sleeves. Sew side and sleeve seams.

WOMEN'S VERSION

SIZES

Sized for Small (Medium, Large). Shown in size Small.

FINISHED MEASUREMENTS

■ Bust (buttoned) 36 (39, 41¹/₄)"/91.5 (99, 104.5)cm
■ Length 26 (26¹/₂, 27)"/66 (67.5, 68.5)cm
■ Upper arm 17 (18, 19)"/43 (46, 48)cm

GAUGE

23 sts and 29 rows to 4"/10cm over St st using size 6 (4mm) needles.
TAKE TIME TO CHECK YOUR GAUGE.

STITCHES USED

Stripe pat for body

Work in St st (k on RS, p on WS) in foll color sequence: *2 rows B, 3 rows C, 2 rows B, 6 rows A, 1 row D, [3 rows E, 1 row D] twice, 6 rows A, 2 rows C, 1 row B, 2 rows E, 1 row B, 2 rows C, 6 rows A; rep from * (42 rows) for Stripe pat for body.

Stripe pat for sleeve

Work in St st as foll: *1 row A, 1 row D, [3 rows E, 1 row D] twice, 6 rows A, 2 rows C, 1 row B, 2 rows E, 1 row B, 2 rows C, 6 rows A, 2 rows B, 3 rows C, 2 rows B, 5 rows A; rep from * (42 rows) for Stripe pat for sleeve.

BACK

With A, cast on 103 (111, 119) sts. Work in k1, p1 rib for 1¹/₂"/4cm, end with a RS row. P 1 row. Work Stripe pat for body until piece measures 25 (25¹/₂, 26)"/63.5 (65, 66)cm from beg, end with a WS row.

Shoulder shaping

Bind off 8 (9, 10) sts at beg of next 4 (6, 4) rows, 9 (10, 10) sts at beg of next 4 (2, 4) rows. Bind off rem 35 (37, 39) sts.

Pocket Linings

(Make 2)
With A, cast on 27 sts. Work in St st until piece measures 5"/12.5cm, end with a WS row. Place sts on a holder.

Left Front

With A, cast on 47 (51, 55) sts. Work in k1, p1 rib for 1¹/₂"/4cm, end with a RS row. P 1 row. Work first 36 rows of Stripe pat for body. Piece measures approx 6¹/₂"/16.5cm from beg.

Join Pocket Lining

Next row (RS) Cont pat, k10 (12, 14), sl next 27 sts onto holder, k across 27 sts of pocket lining, k to end of row. Work even until piece measures 23¹/₂ (24, 24¹/₂)"/59.5 (61, 62)cm from beg, end with a RS row.

Neck shaping

Next row (WS) Bind off 5 sts (neck edge), work to end. Cont to bind off at neck edge 3 sts once, 2 sts 1 (1, 2) times. Dec 1 st at neck edge on next row, then every other row 2 (3, 2) times more. AT SAME TIME, when same length as back to shoulder, shape shoulder at beg og RS rows as for back.

RIGHT FRONT

Work to correspond to left front, reversing shaping.

SLEEVES

With A, cast on 55 (57, 61) sts. Work in k1, p1 rib for 1¹/₂"/4cm, end with a RS row. P 1 row. Work Stripe pat for sleeve, AT SAME TIME, inc 1 st each side on 5th row, then every 4th row 6 (9, 10) times more, every 6th row 14 (13, 13) times—97 (103, 109) sts. Work even until piece measures 18 (19, 19¹/₂)"/46 (48, 49.5)cm from beg. Bind off all sts.

FINISHING

Block pieces. Sew shoulder seams.

Neckband

With RS facing and A, beg at right front neck edge pick up and k 81 (83, 85) sts evenly around neck edge. Work in k1, p1 rib for 1"/2.5cm. Bind off all sts in rib.

Buttonband

With RS facing and A, beg at top of neckband, pick up and k 128 (130, 132) sts evenly along left front edge. Work in k1, p1 rib for 1¹/₂"/4cm. Bind off in rib. Place markers along band for 7 buttons, with the first and last ¹/₂"/1.25cm from top and lower edges, and 5 others spaced evenly between.

Buttonhole band

Work to correspond to buttonband, working buttonholes opposite stitch markers when band measures ³/₄"/2cm as foll: bind off 3 sts for each buttonhole; on foll row, cast on 3 sts over each set of bound-off sts.

Pocket edges

With RS facing and A, pick up and k 27 sts from pocket holder. Work in k1, p1 rib for 1"/2.5cm. Bind off in rib. Place markers 8¹/₂ (9, 9¹/₂)"/21.5 (23, 24)cm down from shoulders on front and back for armholes. Sew sleeves between markers. Sew side and sleeve seams. Sew pocket edges to RS of fronts and sew pocket linings to WS. Sew on buttons.

CHILD'S SWEATER

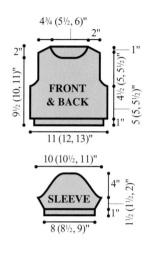

4¾ (5½, 6)"

2"

2"

1"

9½ (10, 11)"

FRONT & BACK

4½ (5, 5½)"

5 (5, 5½)"

1"

11 (12, 13)"

10 (10½, 11)"

SLEEVE

4"

1"

1½ (1½, 2)"

8 (8½, 9)"

WOMEN'S SWEATER

6 (6½, 6¾)"

6 (6½, 7)"

1"

BACK

8½ (9, 9½)"

26 (26½, 27)"

15"

18 (19½, 20¾)"

1½"

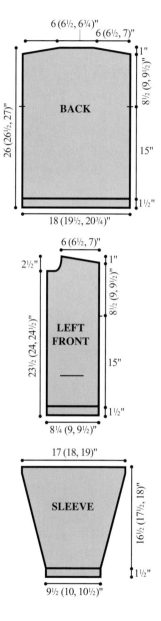

6 (6½, 7)"

2½"

1"

LEFT FRONT

8½ (9, 9½)"

23½ (24, 24½)"

15"

1½"

8¼ (9, 9½)"

17 (18, 19)"

SLEEVE

16½ (17½, 18)"

1½"

9½ (10, 10½)"

Pattern Play

for intermediate knitters

Designed by Susan Mills, casual his-and-her sweaters take you from beachcombing to backyard barbecues. Her notch-collared cardigan and his boxy pullover are worked in a pattern of knit-and-purl diamonds, alternating seed-stitch ribs and purl-stitch crosses. "Pattern Play" first appeared in the Spring/Summer '00 issue of *Family Circle Easy Knitting* magazine.

MATERIALS

- *Cabana* by Reynolds/JCA, 3½oz/100g balls, each approx 135yd/124m (cotton/acrylic)

Women's version

9 (9, 10) balls in #927 blue

Men's version

10 (10, 11) balls in #905 sand

- Five 1"/25mm buttons
- Size 9 (5.5mm) circular needle, 16"/40cm long

Both Versions

- One pair size 10 (6mm) needles OR SIZE TO OBTAIN GAUGE
- Stitch holders

SIZES

Women's version

Sized for Women's Small/Medium (Large/X-Large, XX-Large). Shown in size Large/X-Large.

Men's version

Sized for Men's Small (Medium/Large, X-Large). Shown in size Medium/Large.

WOMEN'S VERSION

FINISHED MEASUREMENTS

- Bust 44½ (47½, 50)"/113 (120.5, 127)cm
- Length 21½ (22, 23)"/54.5 (56, 58.5)cm
- Upper arm 17¼ (18¼, 19)"/44 (46.5, 48)cm

GAUGE

14 sts and 20 rows to 4"/10cm over chart pats using size 10 (6mm) needles.
TAKE TIME TO CHECK YOUR GAUGE.

BACK

Cast on 78 (83, 88) sts.

Beg chart 1

Row 1 (RS) Work 5-st rep 15 (16, 17) times, end with st 8. Cont to foll chart 1 in this way, rep rows 1 and 2 until piece measures 5"/12.5cm from beg.

Beg chart 2

Row 1 (RS) Beg with st 11 (9, 12), work through st 13, then work 12-st rep (sts 2 to 13) 6 (6, 7) times, end st 4 (7, 3). Cont to foll chart 2 in this way through row 25.

Beg chart 3

Row 1 (RS) Beg with st 3 (1, 1), work 6-st rep (sts 3 to 8) 13 (13, 14) times, end with st 8 (11, 10). Cont to foll chart 3 in this way for 1½ (1½, 2)"/4 (4, 5)cm.

Armhole shaping

Bind off 3 sts at beg of next 2 rows, dec 1 st each side of next row and every other row once more—68 (73, 78) sts. Work even foll chart 3 until armhole measures 8½ (9, 9½)"/21.5 (23, 24)cm.

Neck and shoulder shaping

Next row (RS) Work 24 (27, 29) sts, place center 20 (19, 20) sts on a holder for neck, join 2nd ball of yarn and work to end. Working both sides at once, work 1 row even. Then bind off from each shoulder edge 6 (7, 7) sts once, 6 (7, 8) sts twice, AT SAME TIME, bind off 2 sts from each neck edge 3 times.

LEFT FRONT

Cast on 35 (38, 41) sts.

Beg chart 1

Row 1 (RS) Work 5-st rep 7 (7, 8) times, end with st 5 (8, 6). Cont to foll chart 1 in this way until piece measures 5"/12.5cm from beg.

Beg chart 2

Row 1 (RS) Beg with st 3 (1, 12), work through st 13, then work 12-st rep 2 (2, 3) times, end with st 13 (14, 4). Cont to foll chart 2 in this way through row 25.

Beg chart 3

Row 1 (RS) Beg with st 1 (2, 1), work 6-st rep 5 (6, 6) times, end with st 11 (9, 11). Cont to foll chart 3 in this way for 1½ (1½, 2)"/4 (4, 5)cm.

Armhole shaping

Bind off 3 sts at beg of next RS row (armhole edge), dec 1 st from armhole edge every other row twice—30 (33, 36) sts. Work even until armhole measures 7½ (8, 8½)"/19 (20.5, 21.5)cm.

Neck shaping

Next row (WS) Bind off 4 (4, 5) sts, work to end. Cont to shape neck binding off 3 sts from neck edge twice, dec 1 st every other row twice, AT SAME TIME, when same length as back, shape shoulder as for back.

RIGHT FRONT

Work as for left front reversing pat placement and all shaping.

SLEEVES

Cast on 28 sts. Working charts and centering as on back, foll chart 1 for 7"/18cm, chart 2 for 25 rows or 5"/12.5cm, then chart 3 for 5"/12.5cm, AT SAME TIME, inc 1 st each side every 4th row 14 (16, 17) times, every 6th row twice—60 (64, 66) sts. Cont pat foll chart 3 until piece measures 17"/43cm from beg.

Cap shaping

Bind off 2 sts at beg of next 4 rows, 1 st at beg of next 2 rows. Bind off rem 50 (54, 56) sts.

FINISHING

Block pieces to measurements. Sew shoulder seams.

Collar

With RS facing, pick up and k 68 sts evenly around neck edge. Work in rib pat foll chart 1 for 2½"/6.5cm. Bind off in rib.

Left front band

Pick up and k 68 (68, 73) sts evenly along left front edge. Work in rib pat foll chart 1 for 2½"/6.5cm. Bind off in rib. Place markers for 5 buttons, the first one at ½"/1.5cm from lower edge, the last one at ½"/1.5cm from top edge and the others spaced evenly between.

Right front band

Work right front band as for left front band, working buttonholes at center of band opposite markers as foll: yo and k2tog. Sew sleeves into armholes. Sew side and sleeve seams. Sew on buttons.

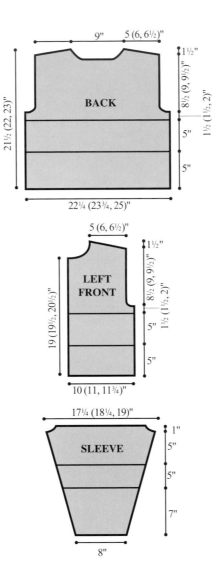

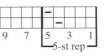

CHART 1

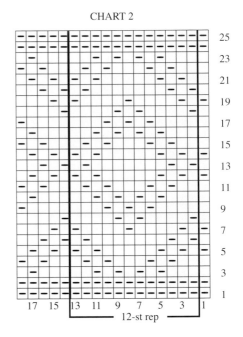

CHART 2

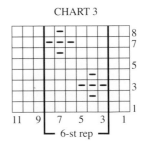

CHART 3

Stitch Key

□ K on RS, P on WS

− P on RS, K on WS

MEN'S VERSION

FINISHED MEASUREMENTS
- Chest 47$\frac{1}{2}$ (50, 53)"/120.5 (127, 134.5)cm
- Length 25 (25$\frac{1}{2}$, 25$\frac{1}{2}$)"/63.5 (65, 65)cm
- Upper arm 18$\frac{1}{4}$ (19$\frac{1}{4}$, 20$\frac{1}{4}$)"/46 (48, 51)cm

GAUGE
14 sts and 20 rows to 4"/10cm over chart pats using size 10 (6mm) needles.
TAKE TIME TO CHECK YOUR GAUGE.

BACK
Cast on 83 (88, 93) sts.
Beg chart 1
Row 1 (RS) Work 5-st rep 16 (17, 18) times, end with st 8. Cont to foll chart 1 in this way, rep rows 1 and 2, until piece measures 11$\frac{1}{2}$ (12, 12)"/29 (30.5, 30.5)cm from beg.
Beg chart 2
Row 1 (RS) Beg with st 9 (12, 10), work through st 13, then work 12-st rep 6 (7, 7) times, end st 7 (3, 6). Cont to foll chart 2 in this way through row 25.
Beg chart 3
Row 1 (RS) Beg with st 1, work 6-st rep 13 (14, 15) times, end with st 11 (10, 9). Cont to foll chart 3 in this way for 7"/18cm.
Neck and shoulder shaping
Next row (RS) Work 31 (33, 35) sts, place center 21 (22, 23) sts on a holder for neck, join 2nd ball of yarn and work to end. Working both sides at once, work 1 row even. Then bind off from each shoulder edge 9 (10, 11) sts twice, 10 sts once, AT SAME TIME, dec 1 st from each neck edge every other row 3 times.

FRONT
Work as for back until piece measures 22 (22$\frac{1}{2}$, 22$\frac{1}{2}$)"/56 (57, 57)cm.
Neck shaping
Next row (RS) Work 34 (36, 38) sts, place center 15 (16, 17) sts on a holder, join 2nd ball of yarn and work to end. Working both sides at once, bind off 2 sts from each neck edge once, dec 1 st every other row 4 times, AT SAME TIME, shape shoulders when same length as back.

SLEEVES
Cast on 33 sts. Working charts and centering as for back, work foll chart 1 for 11"/28cm, chart 2 for 25 rows or 5"/12.5cm, then 2"/5cm in chart 3, AT SAME TIME, inc 1 st each side every 4th row 9 (11, 13) times, every 6th row 6 times—63 (67, 71) sts. When piece measures 18"/45.5cm from beg, bind off.

FINISHING
Block pieces to measurements. Sew shoulder seams.
Neckband
With RS facing and circular needle, pick up and k 63 (65, 67) sts evenly around neck edge including sts on holders. Join and working in rnds, p 3 rnds, dec 3 (0, 2) sts on last rnd—60 (65, 65) sts. Then work pat foll chart 1, working 5-st rep 12 (13, 13) times. Cont in rib foll chart 1 for 2"/5cm. Bind off in rib. Place markers at 9 (9$\frac{1}{2}$, 10)"/23 (24, 25.5)cm down from shoulders. Sew sleeves into armholes between markers. Sew side and sleeve seams.

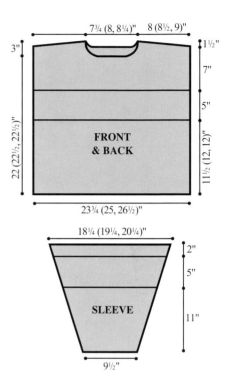

Weekend Special
for beginner knitters

Make some waves in these summer sizzlers. Her vibrant color-block, chunky cardigan features short set-in sleeves and a ribbed collar. His relaxed dropped-shoulder pullover with V-neck showcases bold bands of denium and a rolled hem, perfect for poolside parties or playwear. Designed by Mari Lynn Patrick, "Weekend Special" first appeared in the Spring/Summer'01 issue of *Family Circle Easy Knitting* magazine.

MATERIALS
Women's version
- *Weekend Cotton* by Classic Elite Yarns, 3$\frac{1}{2}$oz/100g hanks, each approx 51yds/47m (cotton)
  5 (5, 6, 6) hanks each in #4832 purple (A), #4858 red (B) and #4885 orange (C)
- Six $\frac{7}{8}$"/22mm buttons

Mens version
  10 (10, 11) skeins in #4893 navy (A), 6 (6, 7) skeins in #4892 lt. blue (B), 6 (6, 7) skeins in #4816 ecru (C)
- Size 11 (8mm) circular needle, 24"/60cm long

Both versions
- One pair each sizes 11 and 13 (8 and 9mm) OR SIZE TO OBTAIN GAUGE

WOMEN'S VERSION

FINISHED MEASUREMENTS
- Bust 35 (38, 41, 43)"/89 (96.5, 104, 109)cm
- Length 22 (22$\frac{1}{2}$, 23, 23$\frac{1}{2}$)"/56 (57, 58.5, 59.5)cm
- Upper arm 12$\frac{1}{2}$ (13$\frac{1}{4}$, 14, 15)"/32 (33.5, 35.5, 38)cm

GAUGE
10 sts and 14 rows to 4"/10cm over St st using larger needles.
TAKE TIME TO CHECK YOUR GAUGE.

Note
When casting on for St st, use single cast-on method on smaller needle. Then change to larger needles to beg working.

BACK
With smaller needle and A, cast on 46 (49, 53, 56) sts. Change to larger needles.
Row 1 (RS) Knit.
Row 2 K1, p to last st, k1. Rep these 2 rows (with a k1 selvage st at each end of row) until piece measures 7$\frac{1}{2}$"/19cm from beg.
Next row (RS) With B, purl (to create ridge). Cont in St st until piece measures 15"/38cm from beg.

Armhole shaping
Next row (RS) With C, bind off 3 sts, purl to end. Cont with C in St st, bind off 3 sts at beg of next row. Dec 1 st each side of next row then every other row 2 (3, 4, 5) times more—34 (35, 37, 38) sts. Work even until armhole measures 7 (7$\frac{1}{2}$, 8, 8$\frac{1}{2}$)"/18 (19, 20.5, 21.5)cm. Bind off.

LEFT FRONT
With smaller needle and A, cast on 27 (29, 31, 33) sts. Change to larger needles.
Row 1 (RS) K23 (25, 27, 29), p1, k1, p1, sl 1 knitwise (for 4-st front band).
Row 2 P1, k1, p1, k1, purl to last st, k1. Cont in this way, rep rows 1 and 2 until piece measures 7$\frac{1}{2}$"/19cm from beg. Cont with A only for front band, work ridge with B, then cont with B until piece measures 15"/38cm from beg.

Armhole shaping
Next row (RS) With C, bind off 3 sts, purl to last 4 sts, work 4-st band with A. Cont with C and front band in A, dec 1 st at armhole edge every other row 3 (4, 5, 6) times—21 (22, 23, 24) sts. Work even until armhole measures 3$\frac{1}{2}$ (4, 4$\frac{1}{2}$, 5)"/9 (10, 11.5, 12.5)cm.

Neck shaping
Next row (WS) Bind off 4 sts, work to end. Cont to bind off from neck edge 3 sts 1 (1, 2, 2) times, 2 sts 1 (2, 1, 1) times, 1 st 2 (1, 1, 2) times. When same length as back, bind off rem 10 sts for shoulder. Place markers for 6 buttons on band, the first one at $\frac{3}{4}$"/2cm from top edge, the last one at $\frac{3}{4}$"/2cm from lower edge and the others evenly spaced between.

RIGHT FRONT
Work as for left front, reversing shaping and placement of front band and working buttonholes on RS rows opposite markers by sl 1 knitwise, p2tog, yo for each buttonhole.

SLEEVES
With smaller needles and A, cast on 29 (31, 33, 35) sts. Cont with smaller needles in k1, p1 rib

for 2"/5cm, inc 1 st each side of last WS row—31 (33, 35, 37) sts. Change to larger needles and cont in St st, inc 1 st each side every 4th row once—33 (35, 37, 39) sts. Work even until piece measures 4"/10cm from beg.

Cap shaping
Bind off 3 sts at beg of next 2 rows, 2 sts at beg of next 2 rows. Dec 1 st each side of next row then every other row 3 (4, 5, 6) times more. Bind off 2 sts at beg of next 4 rows. Bind off rem 7 sts.

FINISHING
Block pieces to measurements. Sew shoulder seams.

MEN'S VERSION

FINISHED MEASUREMENTS
■ Chest 43 (47, 50)"/109 (119, 127)cm
■ Length 29¹/₂ (30, 30¹/₂)"/75 (76, 77.5)cm
■ Upper arm 19¹/₂ (20¹/₂, 21¹/₂)"/49.5 (52, 54.5)cm

GAUGE
10 sts and 14 rows to 4"/10cm over St st using larger needles.
TAKE TIME TO CHECK YOUR GAUGE.

Note
When casting on for St st, use single cast-on method and change to larger needles to beg working.

BACK
With smaller needle and A, cast on 56 (60, 64) sts. Change to larger needles.
Row 1 (RS) Knit.
Row 2 K1, p to last st, k1. Rep these 2 rows (with k1 selvage st at each end of row) until piece measures 9"/23cm from beg.
Next row (RS) With B, purl (to create ridge). Cont in St st until piece measures 18"/45.5cm from beg.

Armhole shaping
Next row (RS) With C, bind off 2 sts, purl to end. Cont with C in St st, binding off 2 sts at beg of next 3 rows. Dec 1 st each side every other row 0 (1, 2) times—48 (50, 52) sts. Work even until armhole measures 10 (10¹/₂, 11)"/25.5 (26.5, 28)cm.

Neck and shoulder shaping
Bind off 5 sts at beg of next 4 rows, 4 (5, 6) sts at beg of next 2 rows and AT SAME TIME, bind off center 14 sts and working both sides at once, bind off 3 sts from each neck edge once.

FRONT
Work as for back until armhole measures 5 (5¹/₂, 6)"/12.5 (14, 15)cm.

V-neck shaping
Next row (RS) Work 20 (21, 22) sts, k2tog, join another ball of yarn and bind off 4 sts, SKP, work to end. Working both sides at once, dec 1 st at each neck edge every other row 7 times—14 (15, 16) sts rem each side. Work even until same length as back. Shape shoulders as on back.

SLEEVES
With smaller needles and A, cast on 23 (25, 25) sts. Work in k1, p1 rib for 2¹/₂"/6.5cm, inc 1 st on last WS row—24 (26, 26) sts. Change to larger needles and cont in St st (with k1 selvage st at each end of row) inc 1 st inside of selvage sts every 4th row 12 (13, 14) times—48 (52, 54) sts. Work even until piece measures 19"/48cm from beg.

Cap shaping
Bind off 2 sts at beg of next 4 rows. Dec 1 st each side of every other row 0 (1, 2) times. Bind off rem 40 (42, 42) sts.

FINISHING
Block to measurements. Sew shoulder seams. Sew sleeves into armholes. Sew side and sleeve seams.

WOMEN'S VERSION

MEN'S VERSION

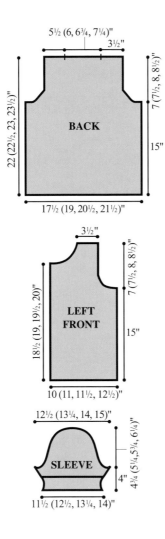

5½ (6, 6¾, 7¼)"

3½"

7 (7½, 8, 8½)"

22 (22½, 23, 23½)"

BACK

15"

17½ (19, 20½, 21½)"

3½"

7 (7½, 8, 8½)"

18½ (19, 19½, 20)"

LEFT FRONT

15"

10 (11, 11½, 12½)"

12½ (13¼, 14, 15)"

4¾ (5¼, 5¾, 6¼)"

SLEEVE

4"

11½ (12½, 13¼, 14)"

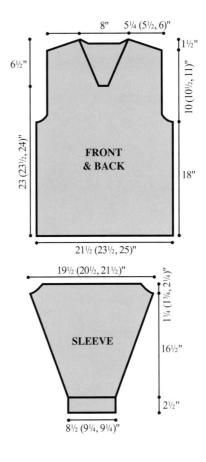

8"

5¼ (5½, 6)"

1½"

6½"

10 (10½, 11)"

23 (23½, 24)"

FRONT & BACK

18"

21½ (23½, 25)"

19½ (20½, 21½)"

1¼ (1¾, 2¼)"

SLEEVE

16½"

2½"

8½ (9¼, 9¼)"

Men of Honor

Snazzy updates turn time-honored classics into must-haves.

Play it Cool

for beginner knitters

Simple rib front detail against a super easy-to-knit stockinette background makes Norah Gaughan's sporty V-neck sweater a winner for a new adventure in a country setting. And the bold blue hue is as sharp as can be. "Play it Cool" first appeared in the Fall '99 issue of *Family Circle Easy Knitting* magazine.

MATERIALS

- *Turnberry Tweed* by Reynolds/JCA, 3½oz/100g balls, each approx 220yd/203m (wool) 8 (8, 9, 9, 10) balls in #32 cobalt
- One pair each sizes 10 and 11 (6 and 8mm) needles OR SIZE TO OBTAIN GAUGE
- Size 10 (6mm) circular needle, 24"/60cm long

SIZES

Sized for Small (Medium, Large, X-Large, XX-Large). Shown in size X-Large.

FINISHED MEASUREMENTS

- Chest 48 (50, 52, 55, 57)"/122 (127, 132, 139.5, 144.5)cm
- Length 25½ (26, 26, 26½, 27)"/64.5 (66, 66, 67, 68.5)cm
- Upper arm 20½ (21, 21, 22½, 23½)"/52 (53, 53, 57, 59.5)cm

GAUGE

11 sts and 17 rows to 4"/10cm over St st using a double strand of yarn and larger needles.
TAKE TIME TO CHECK YOUR GAUGE.

Notes

1 Work with two strands of yarn held tog throughout.

2 Due to the seaming for this extra bulky style, finished measurements reflect sewn pieces, not exact schematic pieces.

BACK

With smaller needles and a double strand of yarn, cast on 68 (70, 74, 78, 80) sts. Work in k1, p1 rib for 2"/5cm, end with a RS row. Change to larger needles and work in St st (beg with a p row) until piece measures 25½ (26, 26, 26½, 27)"/64.5 (66, 66, 67, 68.5)cm from beg. Bind off.

FRONT

With smaller needles and a double strand of yarn, cast on 68 (70, 74, 78, 80) sts. Work in k1, p1 rib for 2"/5cm, end with a RS row. Change to larger needles.

Next row (WS) P30 (31, 33, 35, 36), k2, p1, k2, p1, k2, p to end.

Next row (RS) K30 (31, 33, 35, 36), p2, sl 1 purlwise wyib, k2, sl 1 purlwise wyib, p2, k to end. Rep last 2 rows for pat until piece measures 18 (18½, 18½, 19, 19½)"/45.5 (47, 47, 48, 49.5)cm from beg.

Neck shaping

Next row (RS) K32 (33, 35, 37, 38), join another double strand of yarn and bind off center 4 sts, work to end. Working both sides at once, dec 1 st each side of neck edge every other row 10 (12, 12, 14, 14) times, every 4th row 2 (1, 1, 0, 0) times. Work even on 20 (20, 22, 23, 24) sts each side until same length as back. Bind off rem sts each side for shoulders.

SLEEVES

With smaller needles and a double strand of yarn, cast on 30 (32, 32, 34, 34) sts. Work in k1, p1 rib for 2"/5cm. Change to larger needles and work in St st, inc 1 st each side every 4th row 10 (10, 10, 13, 16) times, every 6th row 4 (4, 4, 2, 0) times—58 (60, 60, 64, 66) sts. Work even until piece measures 19"/48cm from beg. Bind off.

FINISHING

Block pieces to measurements. Sew shoulder seams.

Neckband

With circular needle and a double strand of yarn, beg at left of 4-st center bind-off, pick up and k 82 (86, 86, 90, 90) sts evenly around neck edge, ending at right of 4-st center bind off. Working back and forth in rows, work in k1, p1 rib for 1¼"/3cm. Bind off in rib. Sew ends of rib at center V-neck edge, overlapping left over right neck edge. Fold sleeves in half and sew into armholes. Sew side and sleeve seams.

(See schematics on page 138)

Shift into Neutral

for beginner knitters

Betsy Westman's handsome design is something that can be worn year in, year out, on country jaunts or city forays. Accented with a crochet-edged front notch, the heathered, over-sized pullover draws texture for subtle ribbing. "Shift into Neutral" first appeared in the Fall '00 issue of *Family Circle Easy Knitting* magazine.

MATERIALS
- *14-Ply* by Wool Pak Yarns NZ/Baabajoes Wool Co., 8oz/250g, each approx 310yd/286m (wool)
  3 (3, 4, 4) hanks in heather
- One pair each sizes 10 and 11 (6 and 8mm) needles OR SIZE TO OBTAIN GAUGE
- Size 10 (6mm) circular needle, 16"/40cm long
- Size J/10 (6mm) crochet hook

SIZES
Sized for Small (Medium, Large, X-Large). Shown in size Medium.

FINISHED MEASUREMENTS
- Chest 42 (47, 51, 56)"/106.5 (119, 129.5, 142)cm
- Length 28 (29, 29, 30)"/71 (73.5, 73.5, 76)cm
- Upper arm 20 (21½, 21½, 22)"/51 (54.5, 54.5, 56)cm

GAUGE
12 sts and 16 rows to 4"/10cm over chart pat using larger needles.
TAKE TIME TO CHECK YOUR GAUGE.

BACK
With smaller needles, cast on 63 (70, 77, 84) sts. **Row 1 (RS)** *K4, p3; rep from * to end. **Row 2** K the knit and p the purl sts. Rep row 2 for k4, p3 rib until piece measures 2½"/6.5cm from beg. Change to larger needles.

Beg chart pat
Row 1 (RS) Beg with st 1 (4, 2, 1), work 5-st rep (sts 4 to 8) 12 (14, 15, 16) times, end with st 8 (8, 8, 9). Cont in pat as established until piece measures 17 (17½, 17½, 18)"/43 (44.5, 44.5, 45.5)cm from beg.

Armhole shaping
Bind off 2 sts at beg of next 2 rows. Dec 1 st each side of next row then every other row 1 (1, 2, 2) times more—55 (62, 67, 74) sts. Work even until armhole measures 10 (10½, 10½, 11)"/25.5 (26.5, 26.5, 28)cm.

Neck and shoulder shaping
Bind off 7 (8, 9, 11) sts at beg of next 2 rows, 7 (9, 10, 11) sts at beg of next 2 rows, AT SAME TIME, bind off center 21 (22, 23, 24) sts and working both sides at once, bind off 3 sts from each neck edge once.

FRONT
Work as for back until armhole measures 7 (7½, 7½, 8)"/18 (19, 19, 20.5)cm.

Neck split
Next row (RS) Work 27 (31, 33, 37) sts, join 2nd ball of yarn and bind off 1 (0, 1, 0) st, work to end. Working both sides at once, work 1 row even.

Neck shaping
Next row (RS) Work to last 2 sts of first side, k2tog; on second side, k2tog, work to end. Work 2 rows even. Bind off 5 (6, 6, 7) sts from each neck edge once, 4 sts once, 2 sts once and 1 st once—14 (17, 19, 22) sts each side. When same length as back, shape shoulders as for back.

SLEEVES
With smaller needles, cast on 30 sts. **Row 1 (RS)** K3, *p3; k4; rep from * end last rep k3. **Row 2** K the knit and p the purl sts. Rep row 2 for k4, p3 rib until piece measures 2½"/6.5cm from beg, inc 2 sts on last WS row—32 sts. Change to larger needles.

Beg chart pat
Row 1 (RS) Beg with st 2, work 5-st rep 6 times. Cont in pat as established, inc 1 st each side (working inc sts into pat) every 4th row 14 (16, 16, 17) times—60 (64, 64, 66) sts. Work even until piece measures 20 (20, 21, 22)"/51 (51, 53, 56)cm from beg.

Cap shaping
Bind off 2 sts at beg of next 2 rows, 1 st at beg of next 4 rows—52 (56, 56, 58) sts. Bind off.

FINISHING
Block pieces to measurements. Sew shoulder seams.

Neckband
With RS facing and circular needle, beg at neck shaping above neck split, pick up and k 74 (74, 78, 78) sts evenly around neck edge. Work back and forth in k2, p2 rib for 1"/2.5cm. Bind off in rib. With crochet hook, work an edge of sc around the center V-opening. Sew sleeves into armholes. Sew side and sleeve seams.

(See charts on page 138)

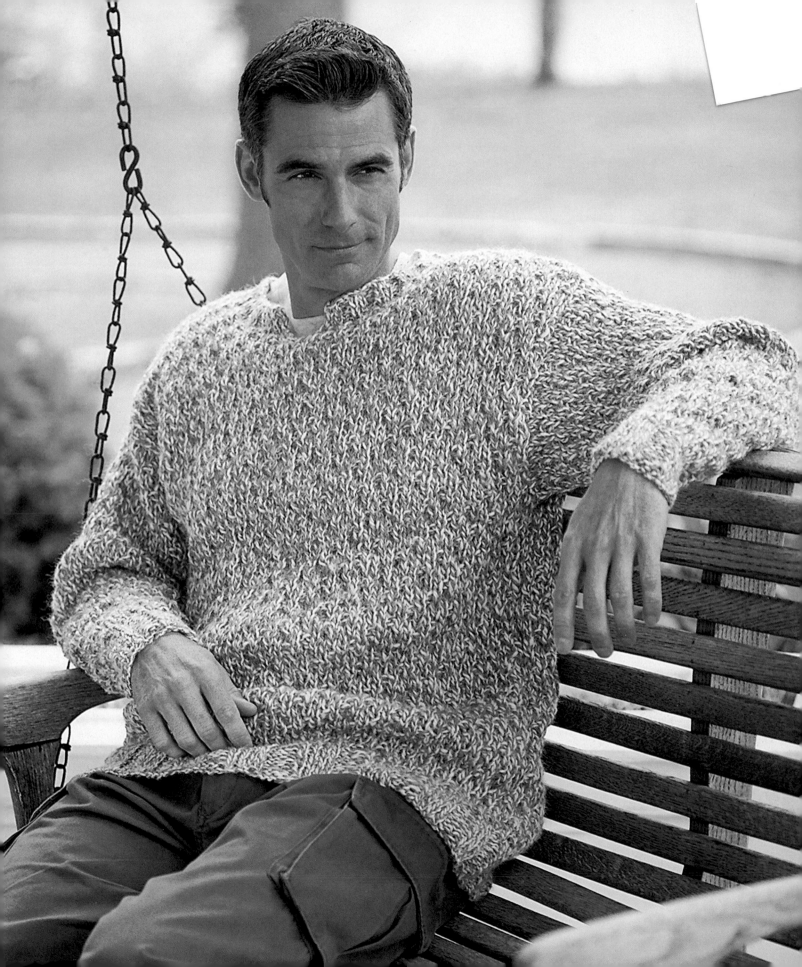

Blue Bayou

for beginner knitters

Coordinating shades of blue make this V-neck pullover a wardrobe staple for any guy. Drop shoulders highlight a decorative diamond pattern across sleeves and upper body while a cable trim adds new dimension. "Blue Bayou" first appeared in the Winter '96/'97 issue of *Family Circle Easy Knitting* magazine.

MATERIALS

- *Cotton Club* by DiVé, 1 ³⁄₄oz/50g, each approx 98yd/90m (cotton, acrylic)
  7(8, 9, 10) balls in # 2707 navy (MC)
  7(8, 9, 10) balls in #1102 light blue (CC)
- One pair size 6 (4mm) needles OR SIZE NEEDED TO OBTAIN GAUGE
- Size 6 (4mm) circular needle, 16"/40cm long
- Cable needle (cn)
- Stitch holder
- Stitch markers

SIZES

Sized for Small (Medium, Large, X-Large, XX-Large) Shown in size Medium.

FINISHED MEASUREMENTS

- Chest at underarm 44 (48, 51, 54)"/112 (122, 129.5, 137)cm
- Length 25 (26, 26¹⁄₂, 27)"/63.5 (66, 67.5, 68.5)cm
- Width at upperarm 16 (17, 18, 19)"/40.5 (43, 46, 48.5)cm

GAUGE

18 sts and 27 rows to 4"/10 cm over St st using size 6 (4mm) needles.
TAKE TIME TO CHECK GAUGE.

BACK

With size 6 (4mm) needles and MC, cast on 96 (108, 108, 120) sts. Work Rib Chart for 8 rows. P 1 row on WS, inc 3 (1, 7, 1) sts evenly across—99 (109, 115, 121) sts. Work in St st until piece measures 14¹⁄₄ (14³⁄₄, 14³⁄₄, 14³⁄₄)"/36 (37.5, 37.5, 37.5)cm from beg, end with a RS row. Purl 6 rows with CC. Purl 7 rows with MC. Beg and end as indicated for back, work Diamond pat chart, AT SAME TIME, after 2 rows of chart have been worked and piece measures 16 (16¹⁄₂, 16¹⁄₂, 16¹⁄₂)"/41.5 (42, 42, 42)cm from beg, shape armhole.

Armhole shaping

Dec 1 st each side on next row, then every other row 4 (6, 7, 8) times more—89 (95, 99, 103) sts. Work even in chart pat until armhole measures 8 (8¹⁄₂, 9, 9¹⁄₂)"/20.5 (21.5, 23, 24)cm, end with a WS row.

Shoulder and neck shaping

Bind off 8 (9, 9, 10) sts at beg of next 6 (6, 2, 4) rows, 0 (0, 10, 11) sts at beg of next 0 (0, 4, 2) rows, AT SAME TIME, bind off center 21 sts and, working both sides at same time, bind off from each neck edge 5 sts twice.

FRONT

Work as for back until ¹⁄₂ (1, 1¹⁄₂, 2¹⁄₂)"/1.5 (2.5, 4, 6.5)cm above beg of armhole shaping, end with a WS row.

V-Neck shaping

Cont shaping armholes at outside edges, AT SAME TIME, place center st on holder and, working both sides at same time with separate balls of yarn, dec 1 st at each neck edge every other row 15 times, every 4th row 5 times. Work even until piece measures same length as back to shoulders. Shape shoulders as for back.

SLEEVES

With size 6 (4mm) needles and MC, cast on 41 (41, 43, 45) sts. Work in k1, p1 rib for 1¹⁄₂"/4cm, end with a RS row. P 1 row on WS with MC. Beg and end as indicated for sleeve, work Diamond pat chart, AT SAME TIME, inc 1 st each side (working incs into chart pat) every 6th (6th, 6th, 4th) row 10 (18, 18, 2) times, every 8th (0, 8th, 6th) row 6 (0, 1, 18) times—73 (77, 81, 85) sts. Work even until piece measures 18¹⁄₂ (18¹⁄₂, 19¹⁄₂, 19¹⁄₂)"/47 (47, 50, 50)cm from beg, end with a WS row.

Cap shaping

Work as for back armhole shaping. Bind off rem 63 (63, 65, 67) sts.

(Continued on page 139)

Stitch Mix
for intermediate knitters

This chunky crewneck brings a new kind of texture to a classic style. Designed by Gayle Bunn in nifty neutrals, it combines various stitch patterns to create a wonderfully different look. "Stitch Mix" first appeared in the Fall '96 issue of *Family Circle Knitting* magazine.

MATERIALS
- *Upcountry* by Patons®, 3½oz/100g, each approx 79yd/72m (wool)
  15 (15, 16, 18) skeins of brown
- One pair each size 9 and 10½ (5.5 and 6.5) needles OR SIZE NEEDED TO OBTAIN GAUGE
- Two stitch holders

SIZES
Sized for Small (Medium, Large, X-Large). Shown in size Large.

FINISHED MEASUREMENTS
- Chest 42 (46, 49, 53)"/107 (117, 124.5, 134.5)cm
- Length 26 (26½, 27½, 28)"/66 (67.5, 70, 71)cm
- Width at upper arm 17 (18, 19, 20)"/43 (45.5, 48.5, 51)cm

GAUGE
14½ sts and 21 rows to 4"/10cm in pat st with size 10½ (6.5mm) needles.
TAKE TIME TO CHECK YOUR GAUGE.

BACK
With smaller needles, cast on 76 (84, 88, 96) sts. RS, work 5 rows in garter st (knit every row). Change to larger needles and p 1 row.

Beg Chart I A
Next row (RS) to establish pat for each size beg chart 1 as follows starting with st 3 (9, 7, 3) work to st 10, rep sts 1-10 across for pat, ending with st 8 (2, 4, 8). Continue working chart thru row 57.

Beg Chart I B
Row 58 (WS) p across. **Row 59 (RS)** start at st 5 (1, 5, 1) work to st 6, rep sts 1-6, ending with 2 (6, 2, 6). Rep Chart I A work until piece measures 26 (26½, 27½, 28). Bind off 25 (29, 30, 33) sts, sl next 26 (26, 28, 30) sts onto a holder, join yarn to next st and bind off rem 25 (29, 30, 33) sts.

FRONT
Work from ** to ** as given for back. Change to larger needles and work Chart 1A and 1B as est, until piece measures 23(23½, 24½,25)"/58.5(60, 62.5, 63.5)cm end with WS row.

Neck shaping
Next row Pat across 32 (36, 37, 41) sts (neck edge), place rem sts on a stitch holders. Cont to foll chart, dec 1 st at neck edge on next 4 rows, then on foll 3 (3, 3, 4) alt rows—25 (29, 30, 33) sts. Work 7 (9, 7, 7) rows even foll chart, ending with a WS row. Bind off. With RS facing, leave center 12 (12, 14, 14) sts on stitch holders, sl rem sts onto needle, join yarn to rem sts at neck edge and pat from chart to end of row. Cont to foll chart, dec 1 st at neck edge on next 4 rows, then on foll 3 (3, 3, 4) alt rows—25 (29, 30, 33) sts. Work until piece measures same as back to shoulder, ending with a WS row. Bind off.

SLEEVES
With smaller needles cast on 38 (40, 40, 42) sts. Beg on WS, work 5 rows in garter st inc 2 sts evenly across last row—40 (42, 42, 44) sts. Change to larger needles. Note: work all inc in pat. Beg chart at st 1 (10, 10, 9) work to st 10, rep chart from 1-10 across for pat, ending with st 10 (1, 1, 2). Cont working charts and inc 1st at each end on 5th row and every foll 4th row until there are 48 (54, 60, 68) sts, then every foll 6th row until there are 68 (72, 76, 80) sts. Work 11 (11, 9, 15) rows even foll chart. Bind off.

FINISHING
Sew right shoulder seam. **Neckband** With RS facing and smaller needles, pick up and k 14 (16, 16, 18) sts down left front neck edge, knit across 12 (12, 14, 14) sts from front st holder, pick up and k 14 (16, 16, 18) sts up right front neck edge, k across 26 (26, 28, 30) sts from back st holder dec 1 st at center—65 (69, 73, 79) sts. Work 4 rows in garter st. Bind off in Knit on WS. Sew left shoulder and neckband seam. Place markers on front and back side edges 9½ (10, 10½, 11)"/24 (25.5, 26.5, 28)cm down from shoulder seams. Sew in sleeves between markers. Sew side and sleeve seams.

(See charts and schematics on page 140)

Checkered Charm

for intermediate knitters

Color, pattern, texture–this cardigan has it all. Designed by Dawn Brocco, this shawl-collar winner boasts checks in harvest shades. "Checkered Charm" first appeared in the Fall '96 issue of *Family Circle Knitting* magazine.

MATERIALS

- *Donegal Tweed* by Tahki Yarns, 3½oz/100g, each approx 183yd/ 169m (wool)
  - 5 (6, 7) balls #880 brick
  - 3 (4, 5) balls #877 honey
- Size 8 (5mm) circular needles 16"/40cm and 29"/73.5cm OR SIZE TO OBTAIN GAUGE
- Size 8 (5mm) double-pointed needles
- Six 1¾"/4.5cm wood buttons
- Stitch holders

SIZES

Sized for Small (Medium, Large). Shown in size Medium.

FINISHED MEASUREMENTS

- Chest (buttoned) 43½ (49½, 55½)cm/110 (126, 141)cm
- Length 24 (27, 30)"/61 (69, 76)cm
- Width at upper arm 18 (19¼, 20)"/46, 49, 51)cm

GAUGE

16 sts and 20 rows to 4"/10cm in St st using size 8 (5mm) needles.
TAKE TIME TO CHECK GAUGE.

STITCH GLOSSARY

Seed St

Row 1 *K 1, p 1*, rep between *'s across
Row 2 K the purl sts, p the knit sts across. Rep Row 2 for seed st pat.

BODY

With longer circular needle and MC, cast on 145 (173, 195) sts. Do not join. Work back and forth on circular needle. Work in k 1, p 1 rib for 15 rows. **Next row (WS)** P across inc 23 (19, 21) sts evenly spaced—168 (192, 216) sts. Beg chart and work for 60 (72, 85) rows. Piece should measure 15 (17½, 20)"/38 (44.5,51)cm from beg. Divide for armholes.

Next row (RS) Work 30 (36, 42) sts in pat, sl to a holder for right front, bind off next 24 sts for underarm, work until there are 60 (72, 84) sts for back, put rem 54 (60, 66) sts on a holder.

Back

Cont in pat on 60 (72, 84) back sts for 45 (48, 50) rows. Shoulder shaping Bind off 13 (17, 28) sts at beg of next 2 rows. Place rem 34 (38, 38) sts on holder.

Right Front

With WS facing, join yarn to right front at underarm and cont in pat for 9 rows, end with a WS row.

Neck shaping

Next row (RS) Dec 1 st at beg of row, work to end. Cont in pat, dec 1 st at neck edge every other row 16 (18, 18) times—13 (17, 23) sts. Work even until same length as back to shoulders. Place sts on holder. Bind off sts. Sew right front shoulder to right back shoulder.

Left Front

With RS facing, join yarn to 54 (60, 66) sts on holder and bind off 24 sts for underarm, work to end. Work rem 30 (36, 42) sts to correspond to right front, reversing shaping.

SLEEVES

Note:

Sleeve is picked up from arm edge then worked in round.

With shorter circular needle and MC, beg at underarm, pick up and k 72 (77, 80) sts (approx 3 sts for every 4 rows) around upper (not including bound-off sts) pick up 1 st at bound-off edge, sl 2nd over this st. Turn and est pat on WS row as foll: Small: *P (1 CC, 1 MC) 6 times, 12 MC*, rep between *'s across. Medium: P 1 MC, 1 CC, *12 MC, (1 CC, 1 MC) 6 times*, rep between *'s across. Large: P 4 MC, *(1 MC, 1 CC) 6 times, 12 MC*, rep between *'s around, ending (1 CC, 1 MC) twice; for all sizes: pick up 1 st at bound-off edge in MC and pass second st over this st.
Next row (RS) Work in pat as est to end, pick up 1 st from edge in same color as last st worked and pass last st over it. Cont in est pat filling in the bound-off edge of armhole until all 12 bound-off sts are worked. Join (wrapping to close gap) and work rnds in pat dec 2 sts at underarm on every 5th rnd 15 (16, 16) times – until 42 (45, 48) sts rem. Small: With MC, work 1 rnd in St st, then 15 rnds in k 1, p 1 rib. Bind off in rib. Medium: With MC (k 13, k2tog) 3 times—42 sts. Work in k 1, p 1 rib for 15 rows. Bind off in rib. Large: With MC (k 6, k2tog) 6 times—42 sts. Work in k 1, p 1 rib for 15 rows. Bind off in rib.

Front Bands and Collar

With RS facing, using longer circular needle and MC, beg at lower right front corner, pick up and k approx 64 (74, 82) sts (3 sts for every 4

(Continued on page 140)

Just Kids!

From classroom to playground, spirited knits make great gear for all seasons.

Snowman Sweater

for intermediate knitters

Get your little one ready for frosty days in Amy Bahrt's fun, festive sweater for tots. Cute mitten pockets and snowman add a dash of whimsy; both are knit separately, then stitched on. A snug fitting striped hat completes the set. "Snowman Sweater" first appeared in the Winter '98/'99 issue of *Family Circle Easy Knitting* magazine.

MATERIALS

- *Saucy* by Reynolds, 3½oz/100g balls, each approx 185yd/170m (cotton)
  - 4 (5, 5) balls in #251 royal (MC)
  - 1 (1, 2) balls in #555 green (A)
  - 1 ball each in #361 red (B), #800 white (C), #899 black (D) and #341 orange (E)
- One pair each sizes 5 and 7 (3.75 and 4.5mm) needles OR SIZE TO OBTAIN GAUGE
- Two ¼"/6mm green buttons
- Stitch holders

SIZES

Sized for Child's 2 (4, 6). Shown in size 2.

FINISHED MEASUREMENTS

- Chest 26 (28, 31)"/66 (71, 78.5)cm
- Length 14½ (16, 17½)"/37 (40.5, 44.5)cm
- Upper arm 11½ (12½, 13¼)"/29 (32, 33.5)cm

GAUGE

20 sts and 24 rows to 4"/10cm over St st using larger needles.
TAKE TIME TO CHECK YOUR GAUGE.

SWEATER

BACK

With smaller needles and MC, cast on 64 (70, 78) sts. Work in k1, p1 rib for 1¼"/3cm, end with a WS row. Change to larger needles and cont in St st until piece measures 14½ (16, 17½)"/37 (40.5, 44.5)cm from beg.

Neck and shoulders

Bind off 19 (21, 25) sts at beg of next 2 rows, sl rem 26 (28, 28) sts on a holder for neck.

FRONT

Work rib as for back. Change to larger needles. Work 0 (4, 8) rows in St st.

Beg snowman chart

Next row (RS) With MC, k14 (17, 21), work 36 sts of snowman chart, with MC, k14 (17, 21). Cont to foll chart in this way through row 61. Then cont with MC only until piece measures 12 (13½, 15)"/30.5 (34, 38)cm from beg.

Neck shaping

Next row (RS) K27 (29, 33) sts, join another ball of yarn and bind off center 10 (12, 12) sts, work to end. Cont to work both sides at once, bind off 3 sts from each neck edge twice, dec 1 st each side every other row twice. When same length as back, bind off rem 19 (21, 25) sts each side for shoulders.

SLEEVES

With smaller needles and MC, cast on 35 sts. Work in k1, p1 rib for 1¼"/3cm, inc 3 sts evenly spaced across last WS row—38 sts. Change to larger needles and cont in stripe pat of 4 rows A, 4 rows MC, AT SAME TIME, inc 1 st each side every 6th row (5, 6, 7) times, every 4th row 5 (6, 7) times—58 (62, 66) sts. Work even until piece measures 12 (12½, 12½)"/30.5 (32, 32)cm from beg. Bind off.

FINISHING

Block pieces to measurements. Sew one shoulder seam.

Neckband

With RS facing, smaller needles and MC, pick up and k 72 (76, 76) sts evenly around neck. Work in k1, p1 rib for 1"/2.5cm. Bind off in rib. Sew 2nd shoulder and neckband seam.

Scarf

With smaller needles and B, cast on 5 sts. Work in garter st for 7"/18cm. Bind off. Fold, and attach at fold to snowman's collar.

Note

With smaller needles and E, cast on 14 sts. K 1 row, p 1 row. Dec 1 st each side of next row and every other row 4 times more—4 sts. Cut yarn leaving an end for sewing. Draw through sts on needle and sew up back seam. Join to snowman's face.

MITTENS

(Make 2 pairs)

Right mitten

With smaller needles and A, cast on 24 (28, 32) sts. Work in k1, p1 rib for 8 rows. Change to larger needles and St st stripe pat of 4 rows MC, 4 rows A. Work a total of 2 (4, 6) rows. Beg thumb gusset.

Next row (RS) K14 (16, 18), pm, insert RH needle into right side of st below next st on needle, sl lp onto needle and k it (R-inc), k1, insert LH needle into left side of st 2 rows below st just knit, k1 tbl (L-inc), pm k to end—26 (30, 34) sts. P 1 row. **Next row** K to marker, sl marker,

work R-inc, k to marker, work L-inc, sl marker, k to end—28 (32, 36) sts. P 1 row. Rep last 2 rows 1 (2, 3) times more—30 (36, 42) sts.

Thumb shaping

Next row K to marker and sl sts to a holder, sl marker, work R-inc, k to marker, work L-inc, leave rem sts unworked—8 (10, 12) thumb sts. Work even on these sts in stripe pat for 1 (1$\frac{1}{2}$, 2)"/2.5 (4, 5)cm.

Next row (RS) [K2tog] 4 (5, 6) times. Cut yarn leaving long end. Pull through sts and fasten tightly. Sew thumb seam. Return to sts for hand and k to thumb, pick up and k 1 st at base of thumb, k to end—24 (28, 32) sts. Work even until piece measures 4$\frac{3}{4}$ (5$\frac{3}{4}$, 6$\frac{3}{4}$)"/12 (14.5, 17)cm from beg.

Top shaping

Next row (RS) *K2, k2tog; rep from * to end—18 (21, 24) sts. P 1 row.

Next row [K1, k2tog] 6 (7, 8) times—12 (14, 16) sts. P 1 row.

Next row [K2tog] 6 (7, 8) times. Cut yarn leaving long end and pull through sts at top and fasten. Sew side seam.

LEFT MITTEN

Work as for right mitten, reversing shaping at thumb gusset by k9 (11, 13) sts, pm, R-inc, k1, L-inc, pm, k to end, then cont as for right mitten. Sew two mittens to snowman foll photo. Sew on buttons for eye. Place markers at 5$\frac{3}{4}$ (6$\frac{1}{4}$, 6$\frac{1}{2}$)"/14.5 (16, 16.5)cm down from shoulders. Sew sleeves to armholes between markers. Sew side and sleeve seams.

HAT

With smaller needle and MC, cast on 86 (90, 96) sts. Work in k1, p1 rib for 8 rows. Change to larger needles and cont in stripe pat of 4 rows A, 4

rows MC, until piece measures 4.5 (5, 5.5)"/11.5 (12.5, 14)cm from beg, end with a WS row.

Next row (RS) *K10 (11, 11), k2tog; rep from * 6 times more, k2 (0, 5). P1 row.

Next row *K9 (10, 10), k2tog; rep from * 6 times more, k2 (0, 5). Cont to dec in this way every other row, having 1 less st in rep before decs, 6 (7.8) times more—30 (28,26) sts. P1 row.

Next row (RS) [K2tog] 15 (14, 13) times. Cut yarn leaving long end for sewing. Draw through rem 15 (14, 13) sts twice and pull tightly to fasten. Sew back seam.

Snowman

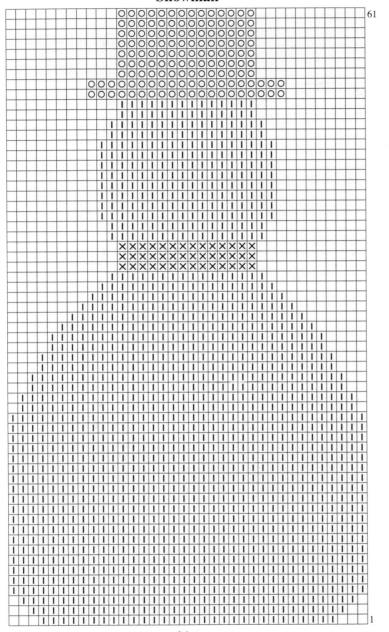

61

36 sts

5¼ (5½, 5½)"

4 (4¼, 5)"

2½"

FRONT & BACK

13¼ (13¾, 16¼)"

12 (13½, 15)"

1¼"

13 (14, 15½)"

11½ (12½ 13¼)"

SLEEVE

10¾ (11¼, 11¼)"

1¼"

7½"

Color Key

☐ Royal (MC)

☒ Red (B)

🇮 White (C)

◎ Black (D)

Shore Thing
for beginner knitters

Norah Gaughan's hooded striped pullover is a cool kid cover-up. A handy button-front pocket lends fun to function; ribbed cuffs, hem, and hood edging add a spirited flourish. "Shore Thing" first appeared in the Spring/Summer '99 issue of *Family Circle Easy Knitting* magazine.

MATERIALS

- *Serenity* by Reynolds/JCA, 1³⁄₄oz/50g balls, each approx 101yd/93m (cotton)
  4 (5, 6) balls in #906 olive (A)
- *Saucy Sport* by Reynolds/JCA, 1³⁄₄oz/50g skeins, each approx 123yd/113m (cotton)
  3 (3, 4) balls in #269 turquoise (B)
- One pair each sizes 4 and 6 (3.5 and 4mm) needles OR SIZE TO OBTAIN GAUGE
- One each sizes 4 and 6 (3.5 and 4mm) circular needle, 16"/40cm long
- Three ³⁄₄"/20mm buttons

SIZES

Sized for Child's 4 (6, 8). Shown in size 4.

FINISHED MEASUREMENTS

- Chest 32¹⁄₂ (34, 36)"/82.5 (86, 91.5)cm
- Length 16 (17, 18¹⁄₂)"/40.5 (43, 47)cm
- Upper arm 14¹⁄₂ (15, 15¹⁄₄)"/37 (38, 39)cm

GAUGE

21 sts and 30 rows to 4"/10cm over rev St st using larger needles.
TAKE TIME TO CHECK YOUR GAUGE.

REVERSE ST ST STRIPE PATTERN

Row 1 (WS) With B, knit.
Row 2 With B, purl.
Row 3 With A, knit.
Row 4 With A, purl.
Rep rows 1-4 for rev St st stripe pat.

BACK

With smaller needles and A, cast on 94 (98, 102) sts. Work in k2, p2 rib working 1 row A, 2 rows B, 2 rows A, 2 rows B, 1 row A. K next row on RS with A, dec 8 sts evenly spaced—86 (90, 94) sts. Change to larger needles and work in rev St st stripe pat until piece measures 16 (17, 18¹⁄₂)"/40.5 (43, 47)cm from beg. Bind off.

FRONT

Work as for back until piece measures 14 (14¹⁄₂, 16)"/35.5 (37, 40.5)cm from beg.

NECK SHAPING

Next row (RS) Work 36 sts, join 2nd ball of yarn and bind off center 14 (18, 22) sts, work to end. Place yarn marker at center of neck. Working both sides at once, bind off 3 sts from each neck edge once, 2 sts twice and 1 st twice. Work even on rem 27 sts each side until same length as back. Bind off.

SLEEVES

With smaller needles and A, cast on 70 (70, 74) sts. Work in rib as for back. K next row on RS with A, dec 4 (2, 4) sts evenly spaced—66 (68, 70) sts. Change to larger needles and work in rev St st stripe pat, inc 1 st each side every 4th row 5 times—76 (78, 80) sts. Work even until piece measures 4"/10cm from beg. Bind off.

FINISHING

Block pieces to measurements. Sew shoulder seams.

HOOD

With larger circular needle and B, beg at center of front neck, pick up and k 92 (100, 108) sts evenly around neck edge. Do not join, but work back and forth in rev St st stripe pat (beg with row 3) as foll: Next row (WS) K2tog, work to last 2 sts, k2tog. Work 1 row even. Rep last 2 rows 7 times more—76 (84, 92) sts. Work even until hood measures 8 (9¹⁄₂, 11)"/20.5 (24, 28)cm from beg. Bind off. Block hood lightly, fold at center back and sew top hood seam. (The bound-off row is hood seam.)

POCKET

With smaller needles and A, cast on 38 sts. Work in k2, p2 rib working 1 row A, *2 rows B, 2 rows A; rep from * until piece measures 5¹⁄₂"/14cm from beg. Bind off in rib.

Pocket flap

With smaller needles and A, cast on 38 sts. Work in rib as for pocket for 5 rows. **Next row** Cont stripe pat, rib 6 sts, bind off 2 sts, [rib 10 sts, bind off 2 sts) twice, rib 6 sts. On next row, cast on 2 sts over each set of bound-off sts. Work even until piece measures 2¹⁄₂"/6.5cm. Bind off in rib. Centering pocket at 3 (3, 3¹⁄₂)"/7.5 (7.5, 9)cm from lower edge, sew to center front. Sew pocket flap at ¹⁄₂"/1.25cm above pocket. Sew buttons onto pocket to match buttonholes. With smaller circular needles and B, pick up and k 102 (118, 138) sts evenly around hood edge. Work back and

(Continued on page 141)

Home for the Holidays

for beginner knitters

The snazzy sweater is edged with embroidered floral trim on the sleeves and diamond-pattern along hem. Celebrate the simple pleasures of the season in Nicky Epstein's cropped pullover. "Home for the Holidays" first appeared in the Winter '00/'01 issue of *Family Circle Easy Knitting* magazine.

MATERIALS
- *Cleckheaton Country 8-Ply* by Plymouth Yarns, 1³⁄₄oz/50g balls, each approx 105yd/96m (wool)
  10 (11, 12) balls in #1102 red (MC)
  1 ball in #3 white (CC)
- One pair each sizes 5 and 6 (3.75 and 4mm) needles OR SIZE TO OBTAIN GAUGE
- Size 5 (3.75mm) circular needle, 24"/60cm long
- Stitch holders

SIZES
Sized for X-Small/Small (Medium, Large/X-Large). Shown in size X-Small/Small.

FINISHED MEASUREMENTS
- Bust 34 (38, 42)"/86 (96.5, 106.5)cm
- Length 20 (20¹⁄₂, 21)"/51 (52, 53)cm
- Upper arm 12¹⁄₂ (14, 15)"/32 (35.5, 38)cm

GAUGE
20 sts and 30 rows to 4"/10cm over St st using larger needles.
TAKE TIME TO CHECK YOUR GAUGE.

BACK

DIAMOND EDGE PATTERN
*With smaller needles and MC, cast on 2 sts.
Row 1 Knit.
Rows 2-10 Cast on 1 st, k to end—11 sts.
Rows 11-19 K2tog, k to end.
Row 20 K2tog—1 st. Place st on holder. Rep from * for desired number of diamonds.

GARTER STRIP EDGE
With smaller needles and MC, cast on a multiple of 10 sts plus 2.
Joining row 1 (RS) K5, k next st tog with 1 diamond from holder, *k9, k next st tog with 1 diamond from holder; rep from *, end k6. Cont in garter st with MC for 9 rows. With CC, work 4 rows in garter st.

BACK
Work 10 (11, 12) diamonds and then with smaller needles and MC, cast on 102 (112, 122) sts and work in garter strip edge pat for a total of 14 rows. Change to larger needles.
Next row (RS) With MC, knit, dec 6 sts evenly spaced across—96 (106, 116) sts. Cont in St st with MC, dec 1 st each side every 10th row 6 times—84 (94, 104) sts. Work even until piece measures 11"/28cm above diamond edge.

Raglan armhole shaping
Bind off 4 (5, 5) sts at beg of next 2 rows.
Dec row 1 (RS) K1, k2tog, k to last 3 sts, ssk, k1. Rep dec row 1 every other row 19 (17, 17) times more.
For Medium and Large/X-Large Sizes only
Dec row 2 (RS) K1, k3tog, k to last 3 sts, sssk, k1. Rep dec row 2 every other row (2, 4) times.
All Sizes Place 36 (36, 38) sts on a holder.

FRONT
Work as for back, including armhole shaping, until 46 (52, 58) sts rem. Cont armhole shaping working dec row 1 5 (2, 0) times more and dec row 2 0 (3, 5) times, AT SAME TIME on next RS row, place center 26 (26, 28) sts on st holder and dec 1 st from each neck edge every other row 3 times. Sl rem 2 sts each side to holders.

SLEEVES
Work 7 (8, 8) diamonds and then with smaller needles and MC, cast on 72 (82, 82) sts and work in garter strip edge pat for a total of 14 rows. Change to larger needles.
Next row (RS) With MC, dec 3 (6, 3) sts evenly spaced—69 (76, 79) sts. Cont in St st with MC, dec 1 st each side every 4th row 8 times—53 (60, 63) sts. Work 9 rows even. Inc 1 st each side of next row then every 8th row 4 (4, 5) times more—63 (70, 75) sts. Work even until piece measures 15"/38cm above diamond edge.

Raglan cap shaping
Bind off 4 (5, 5) sts at beg of next 2 rows.
Dec row 1 (RS) K1, k2tog, k to last 3 sts, ssk, k1. Rep dec row 1 every other row 15 (18, 20) times more, every 4th row 2 (1, 1) times. Sl rem 19 (20, 21) sts to a holder.

FINISHING
Block pieces to measurements. Sew raglan sleeves into armholes. Sew side and sleeve seams. Sew diamond points tog at lower edges.

Neckband
With circular needle and CC, work across 19 (20, 21) sts from left sleeve holder, 2 sts from

(Continued on page 142)

Retro Chic

for intermediate crocheters

Mari Lynn Patrick's granny square pullover is at the head of the class with vintage charm. A funky kaleidoscope of color and slight shaping with square neck and bell-shaped sleeves make this top a stylish winner. "Retro Chic" first appeared in the Spring/Summer '01 issue of *Family Circle Easy Knitting* magazine.

MATERIALS
- *Brilla* by Filatura Di Crosa, 1¾oz/50g balls, each approx 120yd/110m
  - 7 (8) balls in #329 yellow (A)
  - 2 balls each in #310 red (B) and #307 orange (C)
  - 6 (7) balls in #333 turquoise (D)
- Sizes G/6 (4.5mm) and H/8 (5mm) crochet hook for size Small/Medium OR SIZE TO OBTAIN GAUGE
- Sizes H/8 (5mm) and I/9 (5.5mm) crochet hook for size Large OR SIZE TO OBTAIN GAUGE

SIZES
Sized for Small/Medium(Large). Shown in size Small/Medium.

FINISHED MEASUREMENTS
- Bust 39 (42)"/99 (106.5)cm
- Length 21 (23½)"/53 (59.5)cm
- Upper arm 13 (14)"/33 (35.5)cm

GAUGE
Square for size Small/Medium measures 6½"/16.5cm using size H/8 (5mm) hook
Square for size Large measures 7"/18cm using size I/9 (5.5mm) hook.
TAKE TIME TO CHECK YOUR GAUGE.

Note
Five decreased squares are worked with decreases along one straight edge only for lower sleeve cuffs and top of center front neck. For a shorter sleeve than pictured, work 2 squares less at upper arm.

BASIC SQUARE
(Make 24)
With A, and hook for selected size, ch 6, join with a sl st to first ch to form ring.
Rnd 1 Ch 3 (counts as first dc), work 23 sc in ring, sl st to top of ch-3. Cut A, join B in any dc.
Rnd 2 With B, [work 1 sc in next dc, ch 3, skip 2 dc] 8 times, sl st to first sc.

Rnd 3 With B, sl st in next sp, ch 3, 2 dc in same sp, ch 3, [3 dc in next sp, ch 3] 7 times, sl st to top of ch-3. Cut B, join C in any sp.
Rnd 4 With C, ch 3, 2 dc, ch 2 and 3 dc in same sp for a corner, ch 3, 1 sc in next sp, ch 3, * 3 dc, ch 2 and 3 dc in next sp (corner), ch 3, 1 sc in next sp, ch 3, rep from * twice more, sl st to top of ch-3. Cut C, join D in a corner sp.
Rnd 5 With D, ch 3, 2 dc, ch 2 and 3 dc in corner sp, ch 2, [3 dc in next sp, ch 2] twice, *3 dc, ch 2 and 3 dc in next sp, ch 2, [3 dc in next sp, ch 2] twice; rep from * twice more, ch 2, sl st to top of ch-3. Cut D, join A in corner sp.
Rnd 6 With A, ch 3, 2 dc, ch 2 and 3 dc in corner sp, ch 1, 1 dc in center dc of next 3-dc group, ch 1, [1 dc in next sp, ch 1, dc in center of next group, ch 1] 3 times, *3 dc, ch 2, and 3 dc in corner sp, ch 1, 1 dc in center of next group, ch 1, [1 dc in next sp, ch 1, 1 dc in center of next group, ch 1] 3 times; rep from * twice more, sl st to top of ch-3.
Rnd 7 With A, sl st to corner sp, ch 3, 2 dc, ch 2, and 3 dc in same sp, 2-dc group in each of next 8 sps * 3 dc, ch 2, and 3 dc in corner sp, 2-dc group in each of next 8 sps; rep from * twice more, sl st to top of ch-3. Cut A, join D in corner sp.
Rnd 8 With D, ch 3, 2 dc, ch 2 and 3 dc in same sp, ch 1, [2 dc between groups] 9 times, ch 1, 3 dc, ch 2 and 3 dc in corner sp, ch 1, [2 dc

between groups] 9 times, ch 1; rep from * twice more, sl st to top of ch-3. Fasten off.

DECREASED SQUARES
(Make 5)
Rnds 1-5 Work as for basic square. Rnd 6 With A, beg by ch 3, 1 dc, ch 2 and 3 dc, work rnd 6 as for basic square to last side, end 3 dc, ch 2, 2 dc in corner, [ch 1, skip 3-dc cluster, dc in next ch-2 sp, ch 1, dc in center of 3-dc cluster] twice, ch 1, dc in next ch-2sp, ch 1, join with sl st to top of ch-3.
Rnd 7 With A, beg by ch 3, 1dc, ch 2 and 3 dc, work rnd 7 to last side, end 3 dc, ch 2, and 2 dc in corner, work 2-dc clusters in each of next 6 ch-1 sps, join with sl st to top of ch-3. Cut A, join D in corner sp.
Rnd 8 With D, ch 3, 1 dc, ch 2, and 3 dc in same sp, work rnd 8 to last side, 3 dc, ch 2, 2 dc in corner, do not ch-1, work 7 2-dc clusters between each 2-dc cluster, do not ch-1, join.

FINISHING
Block pieces to measurements. Foll diagram for pieces, join 9 squares for back, 8 squares for front and 6 squares for each sleeve with 2 decreased squares at each sleeve cuff and 1 decreased square at center front neck. Join square with D from WS with size G as foll: with

(Continued on page 142)

Sweater Basics

Nothing is more rewarding than a knit sweater for the ones you love. In Family Circle Easy Sweaters, we offer the most enduring and popular styles for you and your family to enjoy. From simple weekend projects to more complex and intricately detailed patternworks, we've designed a collection to accommodate every skill level from beginner to expert.

With over fifty projects to choose from, the exquisite collection features contemporary styles in updated yarns. Don't be afraid to explore your more creative side; indeed we encourage it! Surprisingly wonderful effects can be achieved by simply substituting the yarn or changing the color.

Since clothing measurements have changed in recent decades, it is important to measure yourself or a sweater that fits well, to determine which size to make. Whether you are searching for a "Checkered Charm," for a guy, a "Frosty Sweater" for your child, or a "White Hot" cardigan for yourself, you'll find the perfect pattern in this assortment.

GARMENT CONSTRUCTION

Even though most of the garments in this book are made in pieces, if you are a fairly experienced knitter, you can try knitting many of them in the round, or pick up your sleeve stitches at the underarms and work down to the cuff. You just need to make some simple adjustment to the pattern.

SIZING

Since clothing measurements have changed in recent decades, it is important to measure yourself or a sweater that fits well, to determine which size to make.

YARN SELECTION

For an exact reproduction of the projects photographed, use the yarn listed in the "Materials" section of the pattern. We've chosen yarns that are readily available in the U.S. and Canada at the time of printing. The Resources list on pages 143 provides addresses of yarn distributors. Contact them for the name of a retailer in your area.

YARN SUBSTITUTION

You may wish to substitute yarns. Perhaps you view small-scale projects as a chance to incorporate leftovers from your yarn stash, or the yarn specified may not be available in your area. You'll need to knit to the given gauge to obtain the knitted measurements with a substitute yarn (see "Gauge" below). Be sure to consider how the fiber content of the substitute yarn will affect the comfort and the ease of care of your projects.

After you've successfully gauge-swatched a substitute yarn, you'll need to figure out how much of the substitute yarn the project requires. First, find the total length of the original yarn in the pattern (multiply number of balls by yards/meters per ball). Divide this figure by the new yards/meters per ball (listed on the ball band). Round up to the next whole number. The answer is the number of balls required.

FOLLOWING CHARTS

Charts are a convenient way to follow colorwork, lace, cable, and other stitch patterns at a glance. FCEK stitch charts utilize the universal knitting language of "symbolcraft." When knitting back and forth in rows, read charts from right to left on right side (RS) rows and from left to right on wrong side (WS) rows, repeating any stitch and row repeats as directed in the pattern. When knitting in the round, read charts from right to left on every round. Posting a self-adhesive note under your working row is an easy way to keep track of your place on a chart.

LACE

Lace knitting provides a feminine touch. Knitted lace is formed with "yarn overs," which create an eyelet hole in combination with decreases that create directional effects. To make a yarn over (yo), merely pass the yarn over the right-hand needle to form a new loop. Decreases are worked as k2tog, ssk, or SKP depending on the desired slant and are spelled out specifically with each instruction. On the row or round that follows the lace or eyelet detail, each yarn over is treated as one stitch. If you're new to lace knitting, it's a good idea to count the stitches at the end of each row or round. Making a gauge swatch in the stitch pattern enables you to practice the lace pattern. Instead of binding off the swatch, place the final row on a holder, as the bind off tends to pull in the stitches and distort the gauge.

GAUGE

It is still important to knit a gauge swatch to assure a perfect fit in a sweater. If the gauge is incorrect, a colorwork pattern may become distorted. The type of needles used—straight, circular, wood or metal—will influence gauge, so knit your swatch with the needles you plan to use for the project. Measure gauge as illustrated here. (Launder and block your gauge swatch before taking measurements). Try different needle sizes until your sample measures the required number of stitches and rows. To get fewer stitches to the inch/cm, use larger needles; to get more stitches to the inch/cm, use smaller needles. It's a good idea to keep your gauge swatch to test any embroidery or embellishment, as well as blocking, and cleaning methods.

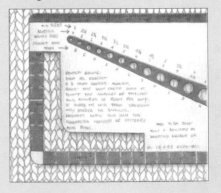

COLORWORK KNITTING

Two main types of colorwork are explored in this book.

INTARSIA

Intarsia is accomplished with separate bobbins of individual colors. This method is ideal for large blocks of color or for motifs that aren't repeated close together. When changing colors, always pick up the new color and wrap it around the old color to prevent holes.

STRANDING

When motifs are closely placed, colorwork is accomplished by stranding along two or more colors per row, creating "floats" on the wrong side of the fabric. This technique is sometimes called Fair Isle knitting after the traditional Fair Isle patterns that are composed of small motifs with frequent color changes.

To keep an even tension and prevent holes while knitting, pick up yarns alternately over and under one another across or around. While knitting, stretch the stitches on the needle slightly wider than the length of the float at the back to keep work from puckering.

When changing colors at the beginning of rows or rounds, carry yarn along for a few rows only, or cut yarn and rejoin when needed. It is important to keep the "floats" small and neat so they don't catch when pulling on the piece.

BLOCKING

Blocking is an all-important finishing step in the knitting process. It is the best way to shape pattern pieces and smooth knitted edges in preparation for sewing together. Most garments retain their shape if the blocking stages in the instructions are followed carefully. Choose a blocking method according to the yarn care label and when in doubt, test-block your gauge swatch.

WET BLOCK METHOD

Using rust-proof pins, pin pieces to measurements on a flat surface and lightly dampen using a spray bottle. Allow to dry before removing pins.

STEAM BLOCK METHOD

With WS facing, pin pieces. Steam lightly, holding the iron 2"/5cm above the knitting. Do not press or it will flatten stitches.

FINISHING

The pieces in this book use a variety of finishing techniques. Directions for making fringes are on page 132. Also refer to the illustrations such as "To Begin Seaming" and

TO BEGIN SEAMING

If you have left a long tail from your cast-on row, you can use this strand to begin sewing. To make a neat join at the lower edge with no gap, use the technique shown here. Thread the strand into a yarn needle. With the rights sides of both pieces facing you, insert the yarn needle from back to front into the corner stitch of the piece without the tail. Making a figure eight with the yarn, insert the needle from back to front into the stitch with the cast-on tail. Tighten to close the gap.

INVISIBLE SEAMING: STOCKINETTE ST

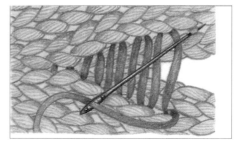

To make an invisible side seam in a garment worked in stockinette stitch, insert the tapestry needle under the horizontal bar between the first and second stitches. Insert the needle into the corresponding bar on the other piece. Pull the yarn gently until the sides meet. Continue alternating from side to side.

"Invisible Seaming: Stockinette St" provided for other useful techniques.

HAND-SEWING

Several items in this book require hand-sewing in the finishing. Use a fine point hand sewing needle and sewing thread that matches the color of the trim. Cut the unsewn ends at an angle to prevent unraveling. When sewing on a trim, use back stitch and keep the stitches small and even.

CARE

Refer to the yarn label for the recommended cleaning method. Many of the projects in the book can be either washed by hand, or in the machine on a gentle or wool cycle, in lukewarm water with a mild detergent. Do not agitate, or soak for more than 10 minutes. Rinse gently with tepid water, then fold in a towel and gently press the water out. Lay flat to dry away from excess heat and light. Check the yarn band for any specific care instructions such as dry cleaning or tumble drying.

BASIC STITCHES

GARTER STITCH

Knit every row. Circular knitting: knit one round, then purl one round.

STOCKINETTE STITCH

Knit right-side rows and purl wrong-side rows. Circular knitting: knit all rounds. (UK: stocking stitch)

REVERSE STOCKINETTE STITCH

Purl right-side rows and knit wrong-side rows. Circular knitting: purl all rounds. (UK: reverse stocking stitch)

DUPLICATE STITCH

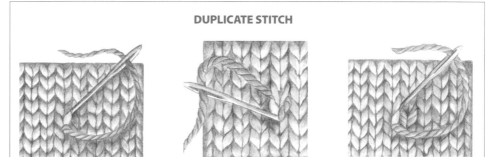

Duplicate stitch covers a knit stitch. Bring the needle up below the stitch to be worked. Insert the needle under both loops one row above and pull it through. Insert it back into the stitch below and through the center of the next stitch in one motion, as shown.

WORKING A YARN OVER

There are different ways to make a yarn over. Which method to use depends on where you are in the stitch pattern. If you do not make the yarn over in the right way, you may lose it on the following row, or make a yarn over that is too big. Here are the different variations:

Between two knit stitches: Bring the yarn from the back of the work to the front between the two needles. Knit the next stitch, bringing the yarn to the back over the right-hand needle, as shown.

Between a knit and a purl stitch: Bring the yarn from the back to the front between the two needles. Then bring it to the back over the right-hand needle and back to the front again, as shown. Purl the next stitch.

Between a purl and a knit stitch: Leave the yarn at the front of the work. Knit the next stitch, bringing the yarn to the back over the right-hand needle, as shown.

Between two purl stitches: Leave the yarn at the front of the work. Bring the yarn to the back over the right-hand needle and to the front again, as shown. Purl the next stitch.

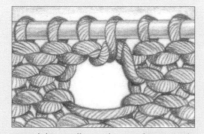

Multiple yarn overs (two or more): Wrap the yarn around the needle, as when working a single yarn over, then continue wrapping the yarn around the needle as many times as indicated. Work the next stitch of the left-hand needle. On the following row, work stitches into the extra yarn overs as described in the pattern. The illustration at right depicts a finished yarn-over on the purl side.

At the beginning of a knit row: Insert the right-hand needle knitwise into the first stitch on the left-hand needle, keeping the yarn in front of the needle. Bring the yarn over the right-hand needle to the back and knit the first stitch, holding the yarn over with your thumb if necessary.

At the beginning of a purl row: Insert the right-hand needle purlwise into the first stitch on the left-hand needle, keeping the yarn behind the needle. Purl the first stitch.

FIBER FACTS

Yarn content plays a big part in choosing your blocking method. Below are recommendations for some common fibers. If your yarn is a fiber blend, choose the process most compatible with the predominant fiber. When in doubt, test on your gauge swatch.

- ACRYLIC Wet block by spraying; do not press.
- ALPACA Wet block, or dry block with warm steam.
- ANGORA Wet block by spraying.
- CASHMERE Wet block, or dry block with warm or hot steam.
- COTTON Wet block, or dry block with warm or hot steam.
- LINEN Wet block, or dry block with warm or hot steam.
- LUREX Do not block.
- MOHAIR Wet block by spraying.
- WOOL Wet block, or dry block with warm steam.

FRINGE

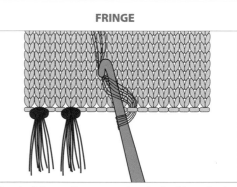

Simple fringe: Cut yarn twice desired length plus extra for knotting. On wrong side, insert hook from front to back through piece and over folded yarn. Pull yarn through. Draw ends through and tighten. Trim yarn.

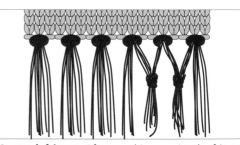

Knotted fringe: After working a simple fringe (it should be longer to allow for extra knotting), take one half of the strands from each fringe and knot them with half the strands from the neighboring fringe.

Knit/Crochet Terms and Abbreviations

approx approximately

beg begin(ning)

bind off Used to finish an edge and keep stitches from unraveling. Lift the first stitch over the second, the second over the third, etc. (UK: cast off)

cast on A foundation row of stitches placed on the needle in order to begin knitting.

CC contrast color

ch chain(s)

cm centimeter(s)

cont continu(e)(ing)

dc double crochet (UK: tr—treble)

dec decrease(ing)–Reduce the stitches in a row (knit 2 together).

dpn double-pointed needle(s)

dtr double treble (UK: trtr—triple treble)

foll follow(s)(ing)

g gram(s)

garter stitch Knit every row. Circular knitting: knit one round, then purl one round.

grp(s) group(s)

hdc half double crochet (UK: htr–half treble)

inc increase(ing)–Add stitches in a row (knit into the front and back of a stitch).

k knit

k2tog knit 2 stitches together

LH left-hand

lp(s) loop(s)

m meter(s)

M1 make one stitch–With the needle tip, lift the strand between last stitch worked and next stitch on the left-hand needle and knit into the back of it. One stitch has been added.

MC main color

mm millimeter(s)

no stitch On some charts, "no stitch" is indicated with shaded spaces where stitches have been decreased or not yet made. In such cases, work the stitches of the chart, skipping over the "no stitch" spaces.

oz ounce(s)

p purl

p2tog purl 2 stitches together

pat(s) pattern

pick up and knit (purl) Knit (or purl) into the loops along an edge.

pm place markers–Place or attach a loop of contrast yarn or purchased stitch marker as indicated.

psso pass slip stitch(es) over

rem remain(s)(ing)

rep repeat

rev St st reverse stockinette stitch–Purl right-side rows, knit wrong-side rows. Circular knitting: purl all rounds. (UK: reverse stocking stitch)

rnd(s) round(s)

RH right-hand

RS right side(s)

sc single crochet (UK: dc–double crochet)

sk skip

SKP Slip 1, knit 1, pass slip stitch over knit 1.

SK2P Slip 1, knit 2 together, pass slip stitch over the knit 2 together.

sl slip–An unworked stitch made by passing a stitch from the left-hand to the right-hand needle as if to purl.

sl st slip stitch (UK: sc–single crochet)

sp(s) space(s)

ssk slip, slip, knit–Slip next 2 stitches knitwise, one at a time, to right-hand needle. Insert tip of left-hand needle into fronts of these stitches from left to right. Knit them together. One stitch has been decreased.

sssk Slip next 3 sts knitwise, one at a time, to right-hand needle. Insert tip of left-hand needle into fronts of these stitches from left to right. Knit them together. Two stitches have been decreased.

st(s) stitch(es)

St st Stockinette stitch–Knit right-side rows, purl wrong-side rows. Circular knitting: knit all rounds. (UK: stocking stitch)

tbl through back of loop

t-ch turning chain

tog together

tr treble (UK: dtr—double treble)

trtr triple treble (UK: qtr—quadruple treble)

WS wrong side(s)

wyib with yarn in back

wyif with yarn in front

work even Continue in pattern without increasing or decreasing. (UK: work straight)

yd yard(s)

yo yarn over–Make a new stitch by wrapping the yarn over the right-hand needle. (UK: yfwd, yon, yrn)

* = Repeat directions following * as many times as indicated.

[ ] = Repeat directions inside brackets as many times as indicated.

KNITTING NEEDLES		CROCHET HOOKS	
US	METRIC	US	METRIC
0	2mm	14 steel	.60mm
1	2.25mm	12 steel	.75mm
2	2.5mm	10 steel	1.00mm
3	3mm	6 steel	1.50mm
4	3.5mm	5 steel	1.75mm
5	3.75mm		
6	4mm	B/1	2.00mm
7	4.5mm	C/2	2.50mm
8	5mm	D/3	3.00mm
9	5.5mm	E/4	3.50mm
10	6mm	F/5	4.00mm
10½	6.5, 7, 7.5mm	G/6	4.50mm
11	8mm	H/8	5.00mm
13	9mm	I/9	5.50mm
15	10mm	J/10	6.00mm
17	12.75mm		6.50mm
19	16mm	K/10½	7.00mm
35	19mm		

Easy Does it

FREE AND EASY

(Continued from page 10)

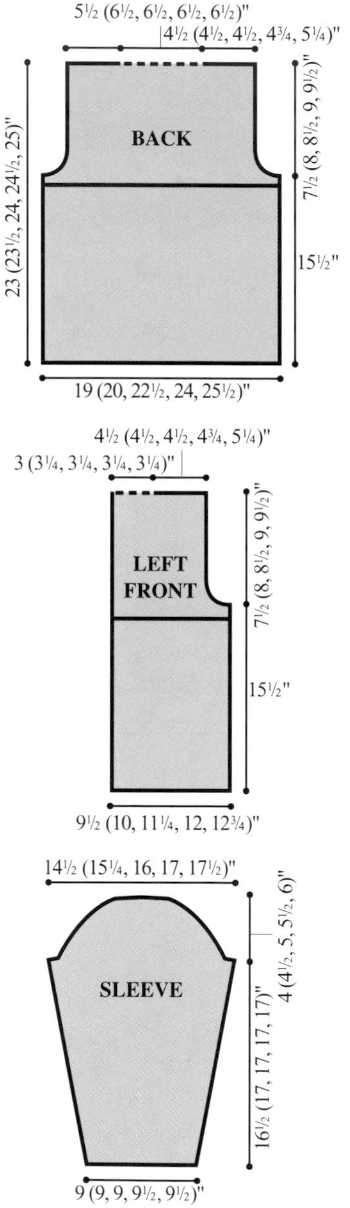
5½ (6½, 6½, 6½, 6½)"
4½ (4½, 4½, 4¾, 5¼)"
BACK
23 (23½, 24, 24½, 25)"
7½ (8, 8½, 9, 9½)"
15½"
19 (20, 22½, 24, 25½)"
4½ (4½, 4½, 4¾, 5¼)"
3 (3¼, 3¼, 3¼, 3¼)"
LEFT FRONT
7½ (8, 8½, 9, 9½)"
15½"
9½ (10, 11¼, 12, 12¾)"
14½ (15¼, 16, 17, 17½)"
SLEEVE
4 (4½, 5, 5½, 6)"
16½ (17, 17, 17, 17)"
9 (9, 9, 9½, 9½)"

LACE NOTES

(Continued from page 24)

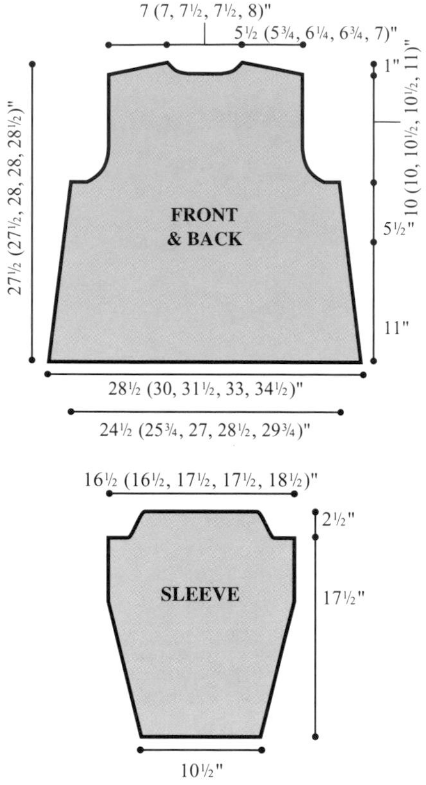
7 (7, 7½, 7½, 8)"
5½ (5¾, 6¼, 6¾, 7)"
1"
10 (10, 10½, 10½, 11)"
27½ (27½, 28, 28, 28½)"
FRONT & BACK
5½"
11"
28½ (30, 31½, 33, 34½)"
24½ (25¾, 27, 28½, 29¾)"
16½ (16½, 17½, 17½, 18½)"
2½"
SLEEVE
17½"
10½"

TEXTURED TUNIC

(Continued from page 8)

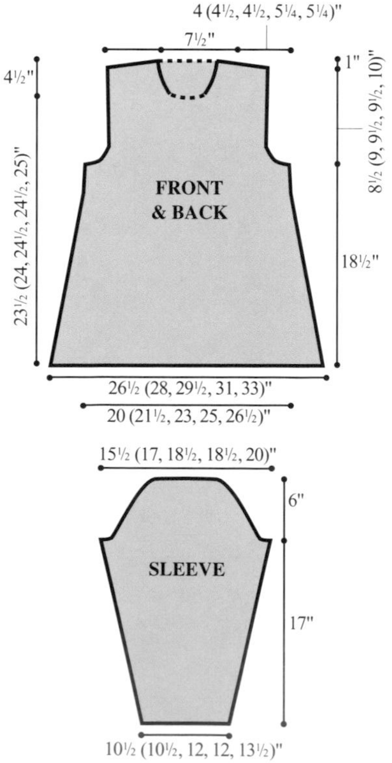
4 (4½, 4½, 5¼, 5¼)"
7½"
4½"
1"
8½ (9, 9½, 9½, 10)"
23½ (24, 24½, 24½, 25)"
FRONT & BACK
18½"
26½ (28, 29½, 31, 33)"
20 (21½, 23, 25, 26½)"
15½ (17, 18½, 18½, 20)"
6"
SLEEVE
17"
10½ (10½, 12, 12, 13½)"

ESSENTIAL CROCHET

(Continued from page 20)

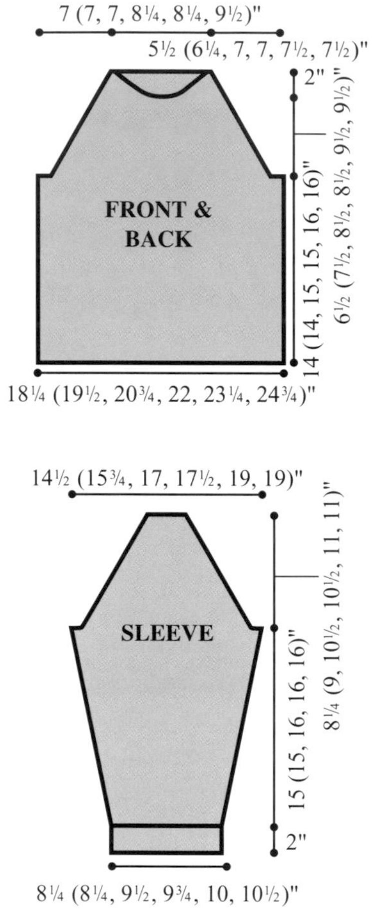
7 (7, 7, 8¼, 8¼, 9½)"
5½ (6¼, 7, 7, 7½, 7½)"
2"
6½ (7½, 8½, 8½, 9½, 9½)"
FRONT & BACK
14 (14, 15, 15, 16, 16)"
18¼ (19½, 20¾, 22, 23¼, 24¾)"
14½ (15¾, 17, 17½, 19, 19)"
8¼ (9, 10½, 10½, 11, 11)"
SLEEVE
15 (15, 16, 16, 16)"
2"
8¼ (8¼, 9½, 9¾, 10, 10½)"

DOUBLE CROSS

(Continued from page 16)

Row 1 (RS) P2 (2, 0, 0), k6 (for 6-st cable), p2, k3, p2; rep from * 1 (1, 2, 2) times, k6 (for 6-st cable), p 2 (2, 0, 0). Cont in pat as established working rows 1-8 of cable pat, AT SAME TIME, inc 1 st each side every 4th row 9 (9, 10, 10) times, every 2nd row 9 (9, 10, 10) times—72 (72, 85, 85) sts. Work even until piece measures 16"/40cm from beg.

Cap shaping

Work same as armhole shaping—62 (62, 75, 75) sts. Bind off.

FINISHING

Pin pieces so that all edges are straight and block to measurements. Sew left shoulder seam. With smaller needles, pick up and k 92

(94, 96, 98) sts evenly around neck. Work in garter stitch for 8 rows. Bind off. Sew right shoulder and neckband seam. Sew sleeves into armholes. Sew side seams leaving last 4¼"/11cm of garter band open for side slits.

CABLE CHART

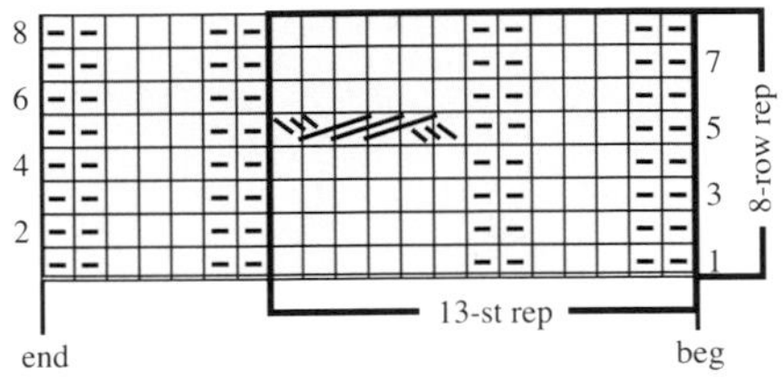
8
6
4
2
7
5
3
1
8-row rep
13-st rep
end
beg

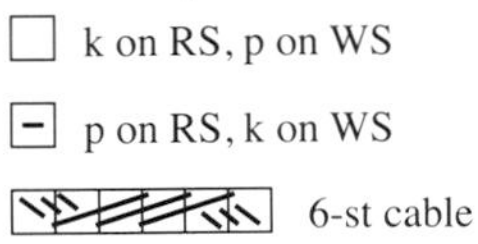
Stitch Key
k on RS, p on WS
p on RS, k on WS
6-st cable

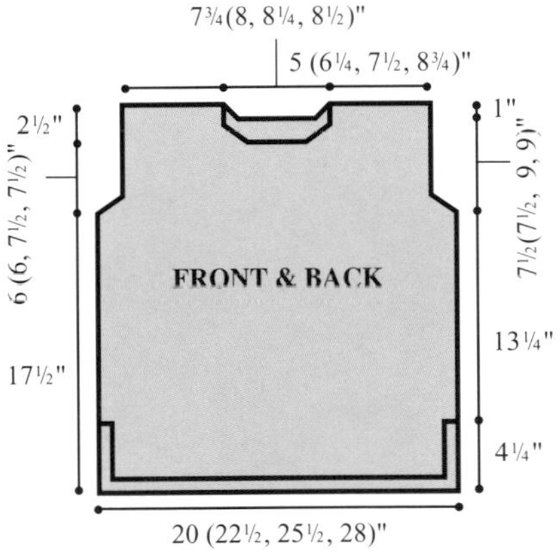
7¾(8, 8¼, 8½)"
5 (6¼, 7½, 8¾)"
2½"
6 (6, 7½, 7½)"
17½"
1"
7½(7½, 9, 9)"
FRONT & BACK
13¼"
4¼"
20 (22½, 25½, 28)"

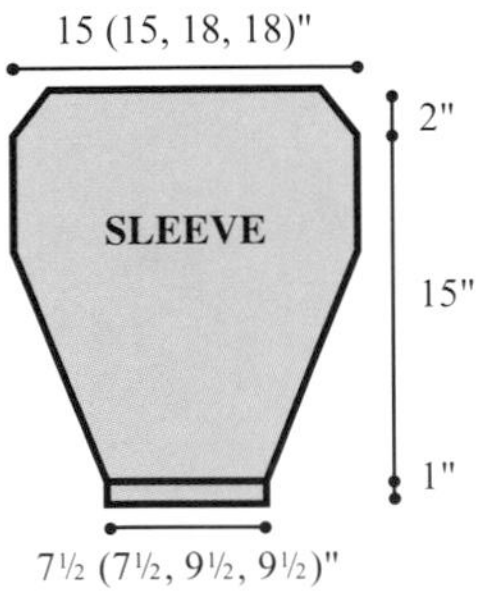
15 (15, 18, 18)"
2"
SLEEVE
15"
1"
7½ (7½, 9½, 9½)"

RED ALERT

(Continued from page 22)

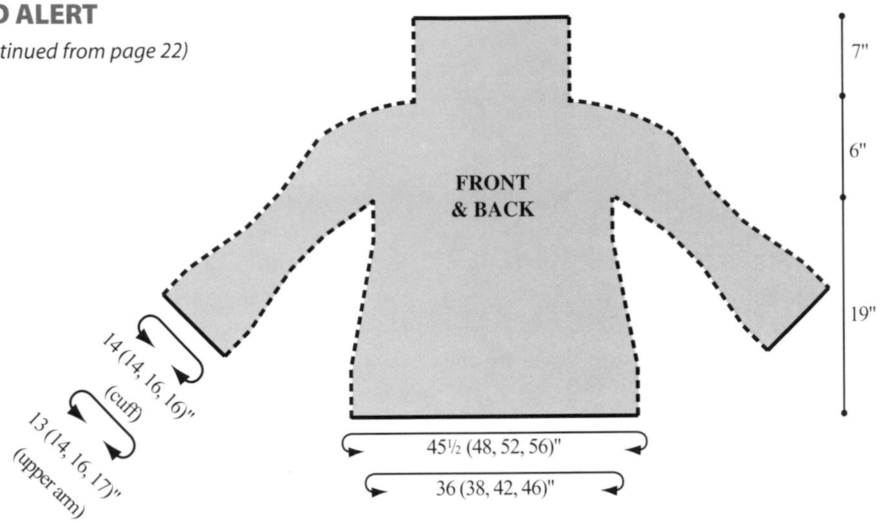
7"
6"
FRONT
& BACK
19"
14 (14, 16, 16)"
(cuff)
13 (14, 16, 17)"
(upper arm)
45½ (48, 52, 56)"
36 (38, 42, 46)"

MODERN CLASSIC

(Continued from page 26)

With smaller needles, pick up and k 20 (22, 24, 24, 26, 28) sts from back neck. Turn. K 1 row. Turn. **Next row (RS)** Knit to end, picking up and k 3 sts at end of row from shaped neck edge, turn. Rep this row 11 (9, 11, 9, 9, 7) times more. Then pick up and k 4 sts at end of next 0 (2, 0, 2, 2, 4) rows—56 (60, 60, 62, 64, 68) sts are picked up (excluding 4-st front bands). Cont in garter st, inc 1 st each side (at 1 st in from outside edges) every 4th row 3 times—62 (66, 66, 68, 70, 74) sts. Work even until collar measures 5"/12.5cm from center back neck. Bind off. Sew grosgrain ribbon to inside of front bands to reinforce leaving 1 st at center free.

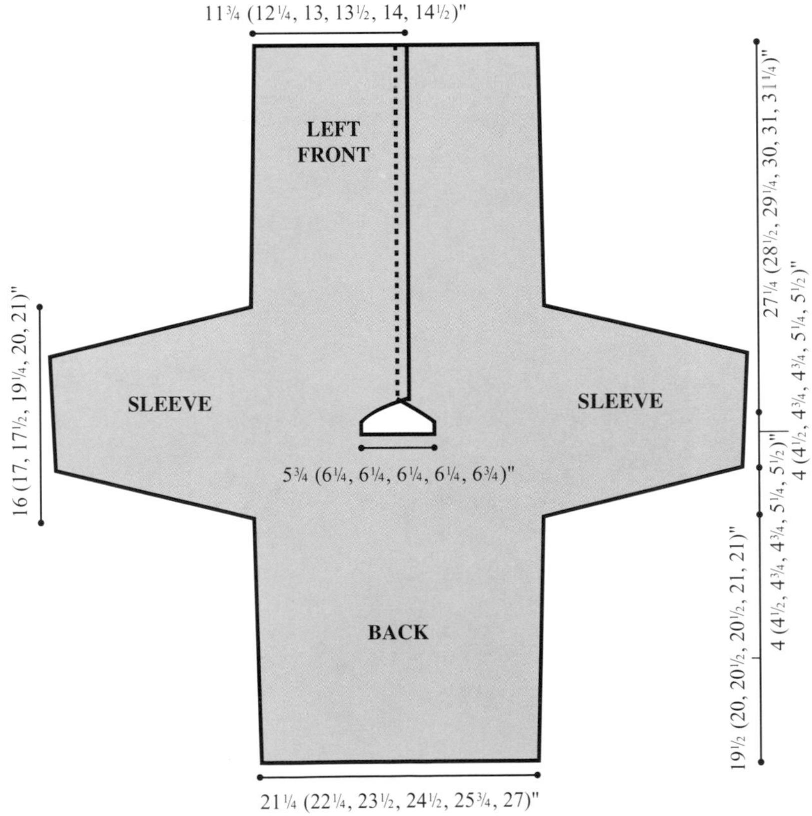
11¾ (12¼, 13, 13½, 14, 14½)"
LEFT
FRONT
27¼ (28½, 29¼, 30, 31, 31¼)"
16 (17, 17½, 19¼, 20, 21)"
SLEEVE
SLEEVE
4 (4½, 4¾, 4¾, 5¼, 5½)"
5¾ (6¼, 6¼, 6¼, 6¼, 6¾)"
4 (4½, 4¾, 4¾, 5¼, 5½)"
BACK
19½ (20, 20½, 20½, 21, 21)"
21¼ (22¼, 23½, 24½, 25¾, 27)"

BIG EASY
(Continued from page 28)

neck and 15 sts along right front neck edge—46 sts. Beg Rib pat on row 2 (a WS row) and work until collar measures 3"/7.5cm. Bind off purlwise on a RS row. Sew in sleeves. Sew side and sleeve seams. Sew buttons on left front band, with the first button 2"/5cm below neck edge, the last button 1½"/4cm above lower edge. Space remaining buttons evenly between. To close jacket, insert button between sts.

COOL CROCHET
(Continued from page 34)

FINISHING
Lower edge
Join with a sl st from RS at lower edge of back and ch 1. Sc in same st with sl st and *(work 2 dc, ch 3, sl st in to 3rd ch from hook, 2 dc) in next ch-2 sp, skip next dc, sc in next dc; rep from * across. Fasten off. Work front lower edge and sleeve edges in same way. Sew shoulder seams.

Neckband
Join yarn at shoulder seam with a sl st and ch 1.
Rnd 1 Work 96 sc around neck. Ch 1.
Rnd 2 Sc in first sc, skip 2 sc, *(2 dc, ch 3, sl st in 3rd ch from hook, 2 dc) in next sc, skip next 2 sc, sc in next sc; rep from * around to last 5 sc, end skip 2 sc, (2 dc, ch 3, sl st in 3rd ch from hook, 2 dc) in next sc, skip next 2 sc, sl st to first sc. Fasten off. Sew sleeves into armholes. Sew side and sleeve seams.

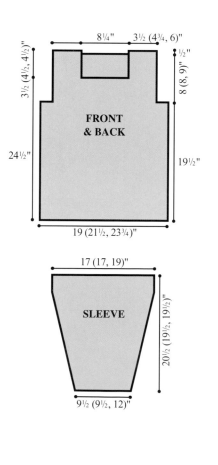

BLOCK PARTY
(Continued from page 18)

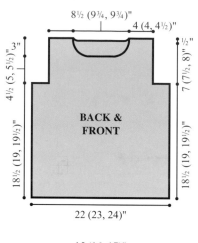

Tropical Coolers

PRETTY IN PINK

(Continued from page 38)

st. Work in rib on 7 sts until band fits along center front edges, then along neck shaping to marker, stretching lightly to fit. Bind off. Place markers for six buttons evenly spaced, having the first one at ½"/1.25cm from lower edge, the last one at beg of neck shaping and the others evenly spaced between. Work right front band to correspond, working yo, p2tog buttonholes to correspond to markers. Sew shoulder seams. Sew bands to neck edge.

COLLAR

With smaller needles and 3 strands of yarn, pick up and k 50 (50, 50, 54) sts evenly around neck edges, beg and end at ends of front band. Work in k2, p2 rib for 2½"/6.5cm. Bind off in rib. Sew six bound-off sts of each band to corresponding 1½"/4cm of collar sides. Sew sleeves into armholes. Sew side and sleeve seams.

Picot edge

With crochet hook and 1 strand of yarn, work edge around sleeve cuffs as foll: Join in seam, 1 sc in joining, *ch 4 and skip 3 sts, sl st in next st, ch 4 and sl st in same st (for picot); rep from * around. Join and fasten off. Work edge along lower edge of ribbing in same way. Sew on buttons.

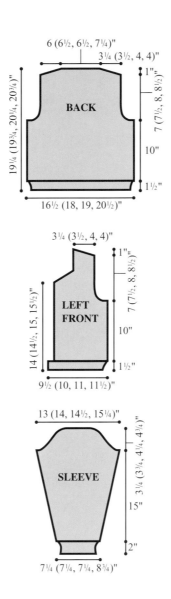

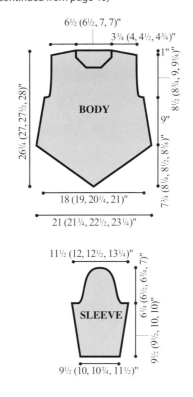

FRINGE BENEFITS

(Continued from page 40)

WHITE HOT

(Continued from page 44)

even until piece measures 13½ (14, 14½)"/34 (35.5, 37)cm from beg, end with a WS row.

Cap shaping

Bind off 3 sts at beg of next 2 rows, 2 sts at beg of next 2 rows, 1 st at beg of next 4 rows. Bind off rem 79 (85, 91) sts.

FINISHING

Block pieces to measurements. Sew shoulder seams. Sew back hood seam, gathering extra fullness. Set in sleeves. Sew side and sleeve seams.

Crochet edging

With RS facing and larger crochet hook, work evenly around entire outside edge of cardigan, including hood, as foll: Work 1 rnd sc, do not turn. Work 1 rnd backwards sc (from left to right). Fasten off. Work in same way along lower edge of sleeves.

(continued on next page)

(cont.)

Twisted cords

(Make 2)

Cut a length of yarn 50"/127cm long and make a twisted cord. Make a knot at 3"/7.5cm from bottom. Thread 3 beads to end of cord. Make a small tassel and attach to end of beads. Attach cords to fronts just under hood.

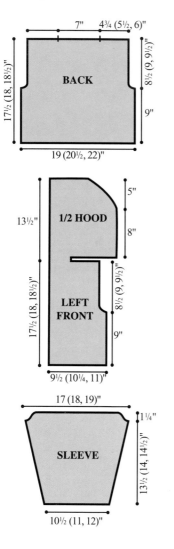

Men of Honor

PLAY IT COOL

(Continued from page 108)

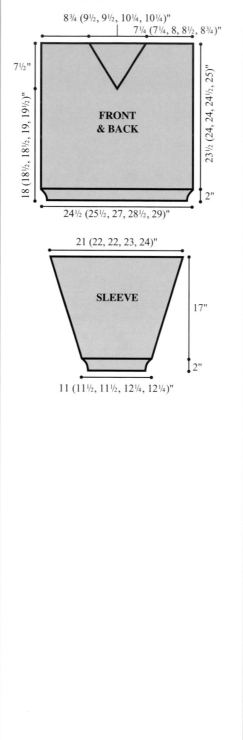

SHIFT INTO NEUTRAL

(Continued from page 110)

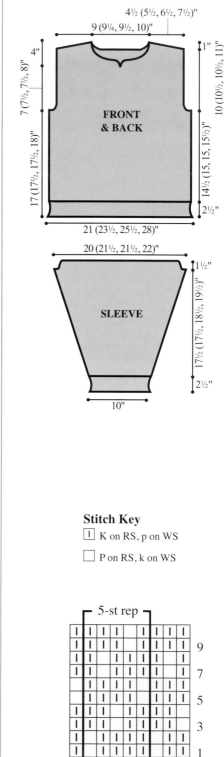

Stitch Key

☐ K on RS, p on WS

☐ P on RS, k on WS

BLUE BAYOU

(Continued from page 112)

FINISHING

Block pieces. Sew shoulder seams.

Neckband

With RS facing, circular needle and MC, beg at right shoulder and pick up and k33 sts evenly along back neck edge, 49 sts evenly along left front neck edge, place marker (pm), k center st from holder, pm, pick up and k49 sts along right front neck edge—132 sts. Place marker, join and work in rnds of k1, p1 rib as foll: Next rnd Work to 2 sts before first marker at center front neck, SKP, k center st, k2tog, then beg with a p1, work in rib to end of rnd. Rep this rnd until band measures 1½"/4cm. Bind off in rib, dec as before. Set in sleeves. Sew side and sleeve seams.

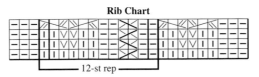

Rib Chart

12-st rep

Stitch Key

☐ K on RS, p on WS

☐ P on RS, k on WS

☑ Sl 1 purlwise wyib on RS; wyif on WS

⧄ 2 RT

⧄ 2 LT

⧄ 3 RC

⧄ 3 LC

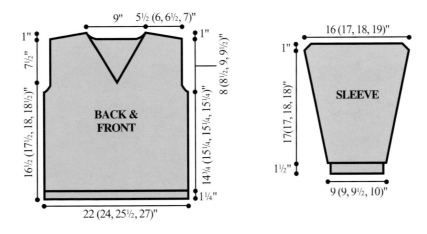

9" 5½ (6, 6½, 7)"

1"   1"

7½"

8 (8½, 9, 9½)"

BACK & FRONT

16½ (17½, 18, 18½)"

14¾ (15¼, 15¼, 15¼)"

1¼"

22 (24, 25½, 27)"

16 (17, 18, 19)"

1"

SLEEVE

17 (17, 18, 18)"

1½"

9 (9, 9½, 10)"

Diamond Pattern Chart

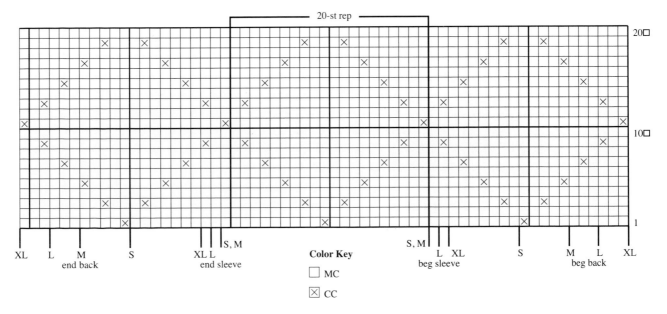

20-st rep

20☐

10☐

1

XL   L   M   S   XL L   S, M   S, M   L XL   S   M   L   XL
end back   end sleeve   beg sleeve   beg back

Color Key

☐ MC

☒ CC

CHECKERED CHARM

(Continued from page 116)

rows) to beg of V-neck shaping, pick up 35 (38, 40) sts to right shoulder, k 34 (38, 38) back of neck sts, pick up and k 35 (38, 38) sts from left shoulder to V-neck, then 64 (74, 82) sts along left front to lower edge 232 (262, 282) sts. Work in seed st for 4 rows. **Next row (WS)** Work six buttonholes (bind off 3 sts for each button-hole, then cast on 3 sts over bound-off sts on foll row) on left front, evenly spaced (approx 10 sts apart) starting 5 sts above lower edge and ending about 2 rows below v-neck shaping. Work 3 rows even in seed st. **Next row (WS)** Work to 37 (40, 42) sts down from right shoul-der place marker and finish row.

Shawl Collar

On next row, work around to 37 (40, 42) sts down from left shoulder, wrap next st, place marker on left hand needle and turn. Work back and forth in seed st pat between markers wrapping at 1 st less on each row 4 times, then 4 less sts on each row 8 times. After last wrap, cont in pat down left side of cardigan to lower edge, covering wraps. Turn and bind off entire edge, covering the rem wraps as you go.

FINISHING

Wet block. Sew on buttons opposite buttonholes.

Color Key
☐ MC
⬜• CC

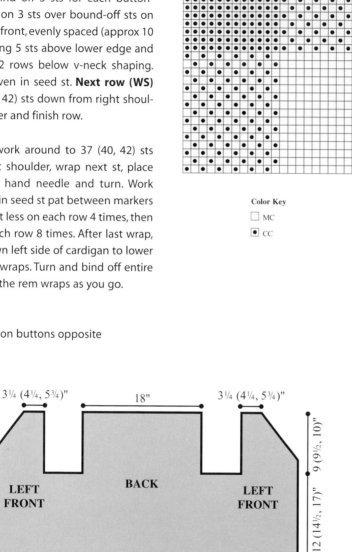

Chart 1A

Chart 1B

Color Key
⊟ P on RS, k on WS
☐ K on RS, p on WS

Just Kids!

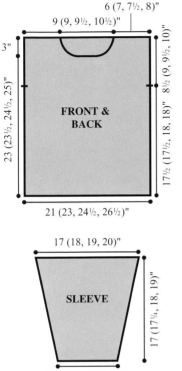

6 (7, 7½, 8)"

9 (9, 9½, 10½)"

3"

FRONT & BACK

23 (23½, 24½, 25)"

8½ (9, 9½, 10)"

17½ (17½, 18, 18)"

21 (23, 24½, 26½)"

17 (18, 19, 20)"

SLEEVE

17 (17¼, 18, 19)"

10 (10½, 10½, 11)"

SHORE THING

(Continued from page 124)

forth in stripe and rib pat until band measures 1"/2.5cm. Bind off in rib. Sew rib to center front neck, overlapping left over right neck edge. Place markers at 7¾ (7½, 7¼)"/18.5 (19, 19.5)cm down from shoulders. Sew sleeves to armholes between markers. Sew side and sleeve seams.

SLEEVES

With smaller needles and A, cast on 70 (70, 74) sts. Work in rib as for back. K next row on RS with A, dec 4 (2, 4) sts evenly spaced—66 (68, 70) sts. Change to larger needles and work in rev St st stripe pat, inc 1 st each side every 4th row 5 times—76 (78, 80) sts. Work even until piece measures 4"/10cm from beg. Bind off.

FINISHING

Block pieces to measurements. Sew shoulder seams.

HOOD

With larger circular needle and B, beg at center of front neck, pick up and k 92 (100, 108) sts evenly around neck edge. Do not join, but work back and forth in rev St st stripe pat (beg with row 3) as foll:
Next row (WS) K2tog, work to last 2 sts, k2tog. Work 1 row even. Rep last 2 rows 7 times more—76 (84, 92) sts. Work even until hood measures 8 (9 1/2, 11)"/20.5 (24, 28)cm from beg. Bind off. Block hood lightly, fold at center back and sew top hood seam (the bound-off row is hood seam)

POCKETS

With smaller needles and A, cast on 38 sts. Work in k2, p2 rib working 1 row A, *2 rows B, 2 rows A; rep from * until piece measures 5½"/14cm from beg. Bind off in rib.
Pocket flap
With smaller needles and A, cast on 38 sts. Work in rib as for pocket for 5 rows.
Next row Cont stripe pat, rib 6 sts, bind off 2 sts, [rib 10 sts, bind off 2 sts) twice, rib 6 sts. On next

row, cast on 2 sts over each set of bound-off sts. Work even until piece measures 2½"/6.5cm. Bind off in rib. Centering pocket at 3 (3, 3½)"/7.5 (7.5, 9)cm from lower edge, sew to center front. Sew pocket flap at ½"/1.25cm above pocket. Sew buttons onto pocket to match buttonholes. With smaller circular needles and B, pick up and k 102 (118, 138) sts evenly around hood edge. Work back and forth in stripe and rib pat until band measures 1"/2.5cm. Bind off in rib. Sew rib to center front neck, overlapping left over right neck edge. Place markers at 7¼ (7½, 7¾)"/18.5 (19, 19.5)cm down from shoulders. Sew sleeves to armholes between markers. Sew side and sleeve seams.

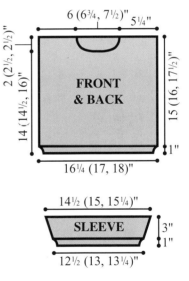

6 (6¾, 7½)"

5¼"

2 (2½, 2½)"

14 (14½, 16)"

FRONT & BACK

15 (16, 17½)"

1"

16¼ (17, 18)"

14½ (15, 15¼)"

SLEEVE

3"

1"

12½ (13, 13¼)"

HOME FOR THE HOLIDAYS

(Continued from page 126)

RS of squares tog, sl st squares tog through 2 inside loops only.

Sleeve edge

With smaller hook for selected size and D, work 1 rnd sc around sleeve cuff edge, join to first sc. Then work 1 sl st in back lps of each sc around.

Lower edge

Rnd 1 With smaller hook for selected size and B, work hdc evenly along lower edge.

Rnd 2 With A, ch 1, *work 1 sc in hdc, skip 2 hdc; rep from * around, join.

Rnd 3 With B, ch 2, work 3 hdc in each ch-2 sp around.

Neck edge

Work 3 rnds as for lower edge, only for each inside corner, yo and pull up a lp in 1 st before corner, yo and pull up a lp in corner, yo and pull up a lp in next st after corner, yo and through all lps on hook.

RETRO CHIC

(Continued from page 128)

left front neck holder and pick up and k 7 sts along shaped neck edge, 26 (26, 28) sts from front neck holder, 9 sts from right front neck as before, 19 (20, 21) sts from right sleeve and 36 (36, 38) sts from back neck—118 (120, 126) sts. Join and work in rnds of garter st (k 1 rnd, p 1 rnd) for 4 rnds. Change to MC and work 6 rnds in garter st. K 1 rnd dec 10 (12, 14) sts evenly spaced—108 (108, 112) sts. Work in garter st for 3 rnds. Bind off.

Embroidery

Work a French knot with CC in center of MC garter bands in every 6th st. Work a 5 petal lazy daisy flower in center of each diamond with a French knot at center.

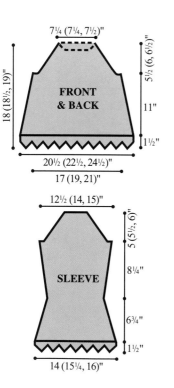

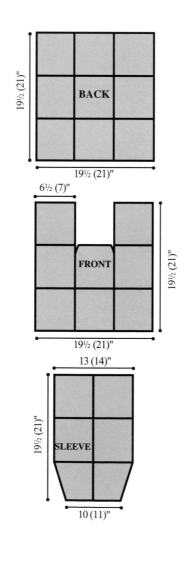

Resources

We have made every effort to ensure the accuracy of the contents of this publication.
We are not responsible for any human or typographical errors.

Acknowledgements

There are so many people who contributed to the making of this book, but most important, we would like to thank the previous editors of *Family Circle Easy Knitting* magazine, including Nancy J. Thomas, Carla S. Scott, Margery Winter, and Gay Bryant. As well, we extend our gratitude to Barbara Winkler, Susan Ungaro, and Diane Lamphron from *Family Circle* for their vision and support. We would also like to extend our appreciation to all of the dedicated and knowledgeable *Family Circle Easy Knitting* staff members, past and present, for their skills and countless hours of hard work in bringing the best of knitting to their readers. Special thanks also goes to the tireless knitters and contributing technical experts, without whom the magazine would not be possible.

Photo Credits

Paul Amato
(pp. 8, 10, 12, 14, 16, 18, 20, 22, 24,
26, 28, 30, 38, 40, 42, 46, 52, 56, 60,
70, 94, 108, 110, 112, 124, 126)

Nick Vaccaro
(pp. 34, 84, 90, 120)

Rudy Molacek
(pp. 64, 74, 80, 114, 116)

Francis Milon
(pp. 44, 98)

Marco Zambelli
(pp. 102, 128)